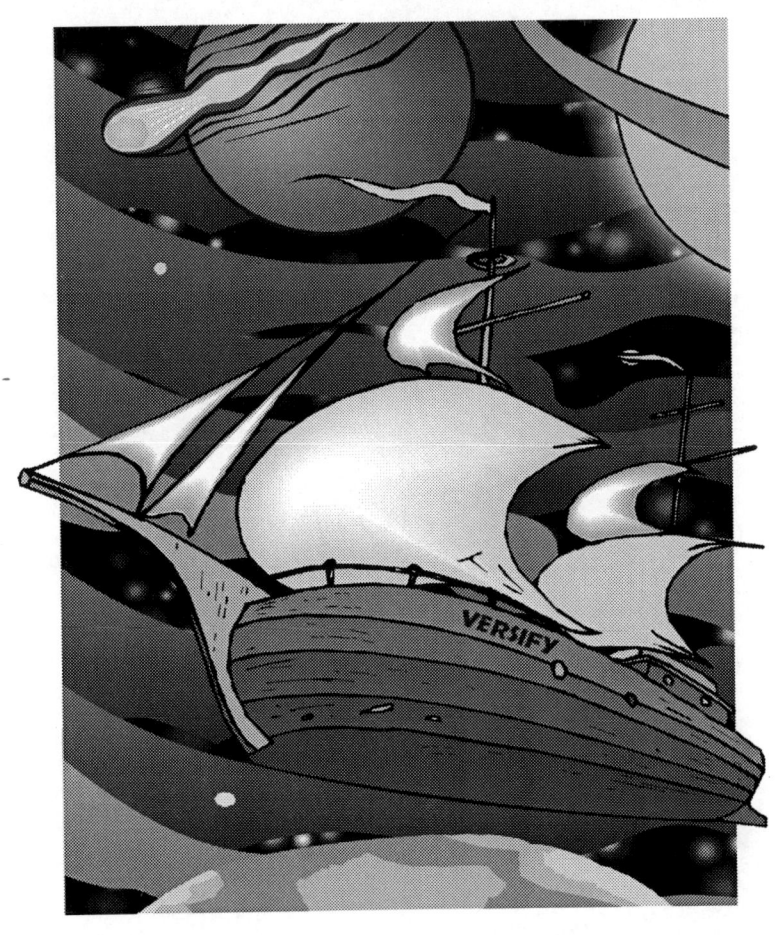

POETIC VOYAGES
WEST YORKSHIRE VOL II

Edited by Dave Thomas

First published in Great Britain in 2001 by
YOUNG WRITERS
Remus House,
Coltsfoot Drive,
Peterborough, PE2 9JX
Telephone (01733) 890066

All Rights Reserved

Copyright Contributors 2001

HB ISBN 0 75433 368 X
SB ISBN 0 75433 369 8

FOREWORD

Young Writers was established in 1991 with the aim to promote creative writing in children, to make reading and writing poetry fun.

This year once again, proved to be a tremendous success with over 88,000 entries received nationwide.

The Poetic Voyages competition has shown us the high standard of work and effort that children are capable of today. It is a reflection of the teaching skills in schools, the enthusiasm and creativity they have injected into their pupils shines clearly within this anthology.

The task of selecting poems was therefore a difficult one but nevertheless, an enjoyable experience. We hope you are as pleased with the final selection in *Poetic Voyages West Yorkshire Volume II* as we are.

Contents

Keely Anne Claire Padgett	1

Ackworth Howard J&I School

Jessica Dobson	1
Emily Jane Storey	2
Sian Hayley Jones	3
Samantha Wassell	4
Charlotte Upex	4
Georgia E Dennison	5
Catherine Farrah	5
Rebecca Lewis	6
Christopher Roughley	6
Philip Eames	7
Charlotte Lunn	8
Alicia Brown	8
Luke Heritage	9
Sophie Mason	10
Hannah Dibb	10
Laura Shutkever	11
Arianne Parkinson	12
Thomas Lister	12
Danielle Askew	13
George Filsell	14

Carlinghow Princess Royal JIN School

Tanya White	14
David William Thompson	15
Jordan Michael Xavier Kennedy	15
Nathan Senior	16
Charlotte Bruce	16
Amber Wilson	16
Jade Lee	17
Leanne Schofield	17
Dominique Delaney	18

Matthew Whitfield	18
Kieran Corbitt	19
Louise Sykes	19
Zoe Ibbetson	20

Cawley Lane JIN School

Amy Vickers	20
Lorna Coates	21
Halimah Nazir	21
Steven Alderson & Nathan McCann	22
Jade Mackay	22
Nabeela Shahzad & Mevish Jamil	23
Tamsin Rounding	24
Kirsty Beverley	24
Alex Swithenbank & Michael Dawson	25
Laviza Nisa-Ali, Kal Bolas, Samantha Coates, Nabeel Hussain & Todd Walker	26
Ola Jegede	26
Ryan Oates	27
Lee Hughes	27
Jack Walshaw	28
Samuel Strand	28
Jade Walker & Leanne Brown	29

Colden Primary School

Greta Wilding	29
Benjamin John Page	30
Ashleigh Louise Tunnicliffe	30
Isabelle McCart	31
George William Emsley	31
Andrea Anderson	32
Lucy Kelly	32
Jake Jackson	32
Taryn Chantal Rath	33
Zoe Cox	33

Sean Luke Smithies	34
Louis Haigh	34
Elizabeth Lamle	35
Andrew Lyons	35
Daniel Edward McCormack	36
Lizzie Johnes	36
Joshua Crawshaw	37
Jacob Clayton	37
Alexander Kay	38

Field Lane Primary School

Jonathan Paul Crossley	38
Richard Strauss	39
Natasha Louise Hrab	39
Cally Scrimshaw	40

Henry Moore Junior School

Stacey Pease	40
Jennifer Lee	41
Lauren Betteridge	42
Laura Feeney	42
Emma Kelleher	43
Ellen McIntyre	43
Georgina Knell	44
Helen Peake	44
Jessica Evans	45
Abbey Winfield	45
Carly Greatbatch	46
Sasha Timson	46
Amy Westerman	47
Laura Cartwright	48
Bradley West Slater	48
Emma-Louise Leeming	49
Stacey-Louise Scott	49
Laurie Kennedy	50
Gemma Louise Scales	50

Jemma Fretwell	50
Martin Duffy	51
Sarah Dyson	51
Eden Spedding	52

Lady Lane Park School

Scott Jessop	52
Rachel Lloyd	53
Daniel Taylor	53
Stuart Slingsby	54
Oliver O'Leary	54
Lottie McDowell	55
Amesh Ahir	56

Lydgate J&I School

Joseph Hathaway	56
Adam Webster & Jason Stott	57
Elmedin Kadiric & Shakil Ahmed	58
Stacie Gelder	58
Ben Helliwell & Dale Smylie	59
Adam Kotia	60
Judd Ledgard & Mark Flynn	60
Becky Barham	61
Marcus Horsley & Nathan Wilkinson	62

Ravensthorpe CE Junior School

Syka Kouser	63
Kristian Nicholson	63
Sonia Hussain	64
Noshaba Butt	64
Annie Wilcock	65
Jeremy Wright	65
Teresa McGrath	66
Sohail Khan	66
Rebecca Hayward	67
Francesca Leona Dec	68
Sam Wilcock	68

Nathan Driver	69
Daniel Paul Hemingway	69
Neelam Uddin	70
Ambreen Hanif	70
Ishrat Zahoor	71

St Anne's RC Primary School, Keighley

Christopher Stead	71
Rebecca Lindley	72
Emma Dodd	72
Andrew Hall	73
Nicholas Smith & Jordan Wise	73
Thomas Gee	74
Lucy Brown	74
Tamara Patti	75
Paul Owens	75
James Gorman	75
Laura Wild	76
Jonathan Taylor	76
Lauren Bilney, Jenifer Beckett & Claire Rowley	77
Josh Fleming	77
Grant Briston	78
Grace Carroll	78
Sofia	79
Alexandra Marie Batty & Allanah Shaw	80
Sam Hill	80
Emma Jayne Cantley & Laura Jayne Lambert	81
David Rhodes	81
Danilo Rocchio	81
Jodie Gorman	82
Jade Charlton & Joshua Payne	82
Katie Hickman	83
Haylie James	83
Sarah Marshall	84
Sian Horsman	84
Christina Cox	85

Kirsty Cummins	85
Adriana Gentile	86
Charlotte Beaumont	86
Luciano Fiore	86
Daniel Mulcahy	87
Zetoon Zafar	87
Jordan Hudson	88
Jacob Driver	88
Luke Hindle	88
Amy Louise Harper	89
Aidan Carter	89
Caitlin Schofield	90
Krystina Murray	90
Jonathan Iwachiw	90
Jonathan Stead	91

St Chad's CE Primary School, Brighouse

Victoria Levy	91
Daniel Wetton	92
Jamie Trolland	92
Cally Harris	92
Callum Curran	93
Elliot Fox	93
Amy Foulds	94
Joe Pritchard	94
Rachael Ward	95
Thomas Polotnianka	96
Jacob Turner	96
Kristofer Gorringe	97
Kate Ratcliffe	97
Reece Smith	97
Andrew Halliday	98
Amy Monday	98
Ben Bussey	99
Richard Mallinson	100
Olivia Green	100

Rory Arnold	100
Emily Jane Crossley	101
Alex Cust	101
Jonathan Lott	101
Joshua Clarke	102

St Francis RC School, Bradford

Luke Friis	102
James Hirst	103
Olivia Leigh Cranmer	103
Emma Wilkinson	104
Adam Butler-Fagbohun	104
Christopher Doonan	105
Megan Harper	106
Michael Friis	106
Marco Rudak	107
Laura Slack	108
Thomas Heap	108
Alexandra Bolland	109
Lauren Robbins	109
Nathalie Mannion	110
Eddie Swales	110
Laura Frances Sheerin	111
Myles Nesbitt	112
Sam Hannam	112
Gemma Fisher	113
Matthew Smith	114
Fiona Nolan	114
Chantelle Craven	115
Bethany Atack	116
Lorna Stokes	116
Lindsay Parnham	117
Luke Flacks	117
Daniel Murgatroyd	118
Benjamin Houlbrook	119
Georgia Narey	120
Rachael Bland	120

Nicholas Doyle	121
Emma Dickenson	121
James Lencki	122
Rory Doyle	122
Georgina Lennon	123
Alexandra Cansfield	124
Nicky Hardaker	124
Rachel Noble	125
Matthew Taylor	126
Rachel Capuvanno	126
Chloe Dores	127
Rebecca Brown	128
Jessica Farrell	128
Christopher Johnson	129
Amelia Crossland	129

St Joseph's RC Primary School, Bradford

Jamie Douglas	130
Nicole Holmes	130
Emily Clark	131
Ashleigh Brooksbank	131
Daniella Baggio	132
Sarah O'Brien	132
Talitha M'Benga	133
Aimée Harrison	134
Hayley Firth	134

St Joseph's RC Primary School, Brighouse

Elizabeth Peel	135
Stephanie Lofthouse	135
Adam James Foster	136
Frances Tomlinson	137
Craig Lee	138
Gabrielle Greenwood	139
Sean McGeady	140
Luke Cowling	140

Scott Morris	141
Emma Hempenstall	141
Jade Haley	142
Kate McBride	142

St Joseph's RC J&I School, Castleford

Kayleigh Harney	142
Lee Dawson	143
Afshan Naheed Lone	143
Christina Sice	144
Daniel Smith	144
Sarah Crossland	145
William Delany	145
Lutangu Sando	146
Francine Hey	146
Paige Tomlinson	146
Richard Dye	147
Adam Hetherington	147
Dale Turner	147
Philip Leigh Newman	148
Stephanie Hetherington	148
Kyle Boyle	148
Aaron Robinson	149
Louise Forster	149
Nicola Louise Newman	149
Nicole Tracey	150
Mariella Tempera	150
Steven Adey	151
Jordan Rice	151
Ian Campbell	152
Adam Brown	152
Lauren Robinson	152
Abigail Skinner	153
Carl Flanagan	153
Becky Thourgood	154
Rebecca Sice	154

Siobhan Coyle	154
Joseph Quinn	155
Matthew Corcoran	155
Matthew Williamson	156
Lauren Sims	156
Joseph Brownridge	157
Christopher Chilstone-Vause	157
Matthew Cogan	158
Joshua Marcus Gray	158

Westville House Prep School

Charlotte Slater	159
William White	159
Kirsten van Terheyden	160
Sam Ashton	160
Harry Fisher	161
Ayman Khokar	162
Rebecca Barnes	162
David Helliwell	163
George Hardy	164
Matthew Riddell	164
Charlotte James	165
Joseph Holloway	165
Alexander Raczkowski	166
Orlando St Clair-Charles	166
Kimberley Howard	167
Jessica Jarrold	167
Sam Macro	168
James Roulston	168
Jonathan Baxandall	169
Joseph Pointon	169
Calum Metcalfe	170
Clem McDowell	170
Richard Mason	171
Harry Kirwan	171
Polly Goodall	172

The Poems

It's Not Fair

It's not fair
Because I'm the only bear.
I always need to smile
Because I'm a crocodile.

I always read many a book
Because I'm a small and quiet duck.
I have to chase every rat
Because I'm a big, fat pussy cat.
I have to jump like a frog
Because I'm a loud, barking dog.

As you can see,
It's not fair for these,
So please don't pick on them
And please don't tease.

Keely Anne Claire Padgett (10)

Pocket Travel

I am going to space
With an undone lace,
I am not going on a rocket,
I am going in a pocket,
I am visiting Saturn
To play with the pattern,
Then it's time to go to Mars
To pick the stars,
I put them in the pocket
And return to Earth by rocket.

Jessica Dobson (9)
Ackworth Howard J&I School

IF I RULED THE WORLD

If I,
If I ruled,
If I ruled the world,

No wars,
More tours,
With a suitcase.

Homes of course
Not for a horse,
But for poor people,
A house that's what they will keep.

Sian helps old people,
(With help) up a money steeple,
All old thank her,
Thank the gardener.

When someone's lonesome,
Sam's got a friend,
Right to the end,
Then they're wholesome.

Arianne another friend of mine,
Takes cares of all the slime,
No more pollution!
That's the solution.

Emily Jane Storey (9)
Ackworth Howard J&I School

I Survived The Titanic

I got out of my car and saw before my eyes,
A ship as high as birds that are flying in the sky,
The ship's name is Titanic; it was new, so very new,
No one had ever sailed on her, not even the crew,
We were told the ship would never sink,
As we sat with the Captain and our 'welcome aboard drink'.

I went for a stroll on deck, to finish my day off nice,
When all of a sudden we hit it, that huge mountain of ice,
People were falling into the freezing cold water,
One woman shouted, 'Please help my daughter'
The crew sent bright flares way up in the sky,
To catch the attention of anyone close by.

The ship then capsized, quite suddenly,
More people were falling into the sea,
I grabbed on a rail, I needed to grip,
I had to make sure that I didn't slip,
The ship capsized more, it was vital I jump,
I closed my eyes and landed with a thump.

I opened my eyes, I was on a table,
I saw people just hanging from wires and cables,
A man came around to see if we were alive,
He honestly thought no one could survive,
I was one of the lucky ones, as I survived,
I remember with sadness, the people that died.

Sian Hayley Jones (9)
Ackworth Howard J&I School

IF I RULED THE WORLD

If I ruled the world . . .
I would make it sunny most of the time,
But I would make sure there would be some rain.
I would not let there be wars or fighting in sight,
I hate to see people in pain.
I would like to keep the Prime Minister
And the Queen just how they are.
I'd make people be kind to each other
(Even brothers and sisters).
I would make it Christmas every month.
I would cut the prices on chocolate, sweets and crisps.
I'd make lollies grow on trees.
I would have pasta every day for my dinner (yum yum!)
I'd make my dad let me have a dog.

Samantha Wassell (9)
Ackworth Howard J&I School

IF I RULED THE WORLD

If I ruled the world,
I would make a rule for no war
And for everyone to get on together,
If I ruled the world,
People would not be able to set up mean websites
And babies wouldn't be able to get sold over the Internet,
If I ruled the world,
There would be peace everywhere
And harmony would echo in the land,
If I ruled the world!

Charlotte Upex (9)
Ackworth Howard J&I School

VOYAGE 2001

On the sea
Sail with me
In a beautiful yellowish boat

With the wind going one way
And no one in my way

On the sea
Sail with me
In a beautiful yellowish boat

I know where I am
And I know that I can.

Georgia E Dennison (8)
Ackworth Howard J&I School

THE JOURNEY TO DEVON

As I sit in the car
While I'm eating chocolate bars
I was really tired
But the trees and houses
I admired
The miles went all day
It was such a long way away
I was still sleepy
But very weepy
The car went on so fast
When we arrived at Devon at last.

Catherine Farrah (9)
Ackworth Howard J&I School

THE SHIP THAT SET SAIL

The ship that set sail all began
In a fairy tail.
Captain Hook was sat at his table,
Reading a map of how to find treasure.

He was also rushing eating his dinner,
His slave came in
And said, 'Shall I sail the boat?'
'No!' said Captain Hook.
'I'm sure I can do it myself,
Don't you?' he shouted.

The slave left sadly,
He said, 'I'm jumping off the ship!
I'm no use here.
If you're not going to need me, so
Bye'
'Bye' said Captain Hook 'Bye.'

Rebecca Lewis (8)
Ackworth Howard J&I School

A JOURNEY TO MY UNCLE JOE'S

Bombing down the motorway to see my uncle Joe
Stuck in London like a piece of dough
'Mum, it takes a long time doesn't it?'
'Of course it does, we're four hours away.'

2 hours to go
Till we get to Uncle Joe's
Down on the M1
Only a short time to go.

1 hour to see my uncle Joe
'Only 1 hour to go Mum.
Isn't it a beautiful view?
All those trees must be new.'

Eventually, we got to Uncle Joe's
'Mum, I've hurt my toes'
'Oh no!' shouted Mum,
'And Daniel's hurt his thumb!'

Christopher Roughley (10)
Ackworth Howard J&I School

A LONG JOURNEY

We were riding in a car,
Going so far!
So far, far away,
Going on *holiday*.

We were talking of a swimming pool,
Thinking how *cool*,
Saying we're going uphill,
Holidays are *brill!*

We were flying on a plane,
It's difficult to explain,
The feeling of excitement,
It was heaven-sent.

We were coming home from Ireland,
Where we heard an Irish band,
It sounded rather simple,
With a smile and a dimple.

Philip Eames (9)
Ackworth Howard J&I School

THE JOURNEY TO THE SUBMARINE

I'm under the sea, swimming like a fish,
Avoiding animals and coral especially sharks.
I'm under the sea, looking at my destination,
A submarine, black as coal and floating at the surface.

I'm under the sea, seeing fish,
With brighter colours than the sub.
It's almost like the sub's not there,
Camouflaged in a way.

I'm under the sea, swimming,
It seems like I'm floating on air,
But with goggles and a diving suit,
I've got all the time in the world to stay here.

I'm under the sea, at my destination,
Better get in quick,
I've not got any air left,
I'm under the sea in a submarine.

Charlotte Lunn (10)
Ackworth Howard J&I School

SPACE JOURNEY

Travelling through space at night,
Might give you a very big fright!

In a spaceship flying round,
Only costs you one pound!

In space, on the block,
We found it was nothing but a rock!

We travelled here, near and far,
Then we found God's bar!

When we had a cup of tea,
Something stung, it was a bee!

We travelled home, far and far,
When we got home, we went to another bar!

Alicia Brown (9)
Ackworth Howard J&I School

IF I RULED THE WORLD

If I ruled the world
I would stop all crime in its prime
I would make sure all offenders did their time.

If I ruled the world
I would catch the criminals
I would feed them on cereals.

If I ruled the world
I would catch all the thieves
I would make them beg on their knees.

If I ruled the world
I would stop all the wars
I would keep the weapons behind locked doors.

If I ruled the world
I would make everyone behave
If not, I would put them in a grave.

Luke Heritage (10)
Ackworth Howard J&I School

MOON ZOOM

This year on my holidays
I'm going to the moon
Up, up and away my rocket will zoom
5, 4, 3, 2, 1, *blast-off*
I sit in my spaceship and watch the stars go by
They shine and twinkle
Like diamonds in the sky
I can see the rings of Saturn and the glow of Mars
I see Pluto and Uranus and millions of stars
At last I've landed on the moon
Bouncing about like a big balloon
I'm off again whizzing away having fun on my holiday.

Sophie Mason (8)
Ackworth Howard J&I School

IF I RULED THE WORLD

If I ruled the world,
There would be no dog boneless, no people
Homeless, no animal eating
And definitely no school uniform,
In fact no school at all, just kidding.
No one will be allowed to shoot animals,
Oh and no school bullies either,
But these things can only happen
If I rule the world.

Hannah Dibb (8)
Ackworth Howard J&I School

THE SPACE ADVENTURE

The green adventurous aliens, Zoo and Zip
Decided to go on a solar system trip.
They set off, their adventure had begun
And then, in front of them, they saw the sun.
It was red and extremely hot,
Poor old Zip nearly burnt his not!
They had to set off very soon
To see the gorgeous, silvery moon
And then they saw Neil Armstrong sprint
Across the moon to make his print.
Then Mars came and caught their eye
It looked so beautiful in the sky.
With white at the bottom and blue at the top
Zoo started dancing and could not stop.
Then Pluto came from behind the mist
It seemed as big as Zip's own fist,
With its different colour range
They hoped it would never change.
Venus then started to come into view
With its silver and beautiful pale blue.
Then Uranus was suddenly there
Floating around in mid-air.
Then Neptune began to rise
It gave the aliens a super surprise.
Saturn came between the others
It is so pretty it's sure to have lovers.
Next came Mercury after all the rest
With its beautiful colours they liked it the best.
Then they sailed past the Earth standing big
And they drifted back home with a merry jig.

Laura Shutkever (9)
Ackworth Howard J&I School

IF I RULED THE WORLD

If I ruled the world there would be harmony and peace
And every hunter wouldn't even kill a beast.
Everyone would have a home to live in
And nothing would be wasted to be put in a bin.

There would be no war
And no breaking the law.
People would walk instead of driving their cars
And would be able to venture to mystery stars.

Out of the adult's world and into the child's,
There would be thousands of sweets in their faraway minds.
There would be no bullying because that's against the law
And even if they did, their bottoms would be sore!

There'd be a lot more to say if I did rule the world,
But let's just call it a day, hey!

Arianne Parkinson (9)
Ackworth Howard J&I School

IF I RULED THE WORLD

If I ruled the world
There'll be no guns,
Poor or bankrupt people,
Definitely no litter!

If I ruled the world
I'll say straight away, less school,
Watch TV all day,
Then get free chocolate!

If I ruled the world
I'd star in the Harry Potter series,
Then play for Man U!
If I ruled the world.

Thomas Lister (9)
Ackworth Howard J&I School

A JOURNEY IN A PLANE

The aeroplane doors are closed very tight
Everyone is ready and waiting for the flight
We get instructions of what to do
Easy to remember because they are few

The aeroplane sets off towards the runway
'Fasten your seatbelts' the sign does say
The engines roar with a glow
We hold on tight, ready to go

The aeroplane sets off at an enormous speed
It zooms along, happy to be freed
The wheels eventually leave the ground
Our destination will be found

The aeroplane flies into a cloud
Engines are roaring and still very loud
Soon we are travelling so straight
The plane still holding our weight

The aeroplane arrives on Earth
We could see lots of people surf
We'll have a good time with lots of fun
Bathing peacefully in the sun.

Danielle Askew (9)
Ackworth Howard J&I School

IF I RULED THE WORLD

If I ruled the world
All the blind would see
All the deaf would hear
All the armies in the world
Would quickly disappear
All the lame would walk
All the ill would be cured
All the empty bellies of the poor
Would be full, I'm sure.

George Filsell (9)
Ackworth Howard J&I School

MY BROTHER

My brother,
A teenager,
Kind, frantic, daring,
Like a bull in a china shop,
A chip off the old block,
I feel lucky,
Like winning the brother lottery,
My brother,
It reminds me how special he is.

Tanya White (10)
Carlinghow Princess Royal JIN School

The Sea

The sea,
Home to plants and fish,
Immense, deep, unpredictable,
As clear as crystal,
Like a blanket covering the Earth,
It makes me feel like a speck of insignificance,
A single grain of sand in the desert,
The sea,
A water world.

David William Thompson (10)
Carlinghow Princess Royal JIN School

The Sun

The sun,
It is 150 million kilometres away,
A ball of fire, motionless, enormous,
As hot as lava,
Like a torch for the world,
It dictates my mood,
When the sun beats down it's like fire,
The sun,
Lightens the doorway of experience.

Jordan Michael Xavier Kennedy (9)
Carlinghow Princess Royal JIN School

FOOTBALL

Football is played by millions of people,
Entertaining, enjoyable, energetic,
Like a ray of sunshine in my life.
I practice as regular as clockwork,
When I score, I feel like a dog with two tails,
Football is the excitement in my life.

Nathan Senior (10)
Carlinghow Princess Royal JIN School

A SHOOTING STAR

A shooting star,
A meteor in the sky,
Bright, fast, twinkling,
Shining like a new coin,
It shoots through the sky like lightning,
I feel as happy as Larry,
The shooting star,
Where does it go when it disappears?

Charlotte Bruce (9)
Carlinghow Princess Royal JIN School

TIGERS

The tiger's stripes are like his prey,
He creeps around every day.
It takes time to find some meat,
His size can be up to five feet.
His teeth are sharper than you can imagine,
If he strikes, it will hurt more than anything.

Amber Wilson (10)
Carlinghow Princess Royal JIN School

MY FRIEND

My friend,
My friend has good humour,
Loyal, trustworthy and kind,
We're like birds of a feather,
Peas in a pod,
I feel lucky to have friends,
Like the cat who got the cream,
My friend,
I am never alone.

Jade Lee (10)
Carlinghow Princess Royal JIN School

MY DOG, BRUCE

My dog, Bruce
Really belongs to Grandad.
Gentle, noisy, giddy,
Like a cart full of monkeys,
Like a ray of sunshine,
I feel we're inseparable,
Like we're joined at the hip.
My dog, Bruce
Will always be there through thick and thin.

Leanne Schofield (9)
Carlinghow Princess Royal JIN School

SPACE

Pluto is like a small piece of Blu-tack,
which is caught in gravity.
The solar system is like electric wires
with balls of steel in different sizes.
Mars is like red sand but colder than us.
The galaxy glitters with its sparkling stars.
Astronauts in space see small and huge planets,
full of brightness but no life.

Dominique Delaney (10)
Carlinghow Princess Royal JIN School

FROST

Frost,
Freezes the ground in winter,
Cold, stiff, hard,
Sparkling like a diamond,
As clear as crystal,
It makes me feel cold,
Frost,
I prefer summer.

Matthew Whitfield (10)
Carlinghow Princess Royal JIN School

STARS

Stars
Are really little suns
Bright, glittery, shiny,
As hot as Hell's fires,
As clear as crystal,
I feel comfortable, warm and relaxed,
As large as life,
Stars
Make me feel like I'm a dull speck compared to them.

Kieran Corbitt (10)
Carlinghow Princess Royal JIN School

WASHING MACHINE

Washing machine
Washing all my clothes.
Quick, bubbly, wet,
Like a whirlpool disappearing into the ground.
I feel like a dizzy Frisbee on a roller coaster ride.
Washing machine
I could never live without you.

Louise Sykes (10)
Carlinghow Princess Royal JIN School

Dolphins

Dolphins are mammals that live in the sea,
Dashing, quick, clever,
They bounce as high as the stars,
They're as quick as a flash of lightning,
They're my favourite animal with their soft skin,
The sight of a dolphin makes me cheerful
As if it was Christmas.

Zoe Ibbetson (9)
Carlinghow Princess Royal JIN School

The Monkey

The monkey was swinging
High and low
And ran to a tree
And hit his toe.

Then he came down
Looking like a silly clown
His mum told him off
And gave him a cloth.

He went to his bedroom
Which made him fume
Then he fell onto his back
Then his mum gave him a smack.

Amy Vickers (8)
Cawley Lane JIN School

SCHOOL'S OUT!

School's out, it's time for fun,
Crazy children run about in the sun,
'Holiday! Holiday!' everyone is shouting,
Off to Blackpool, it's really exciting,
On the beach they just lay,
Lounging about in the sun all day,
Singing children sing 'Hip, hip hooray!'

On the backs of the donkeys they shout and roar,
Ultimate times they had on the shore,
Time for bed, they dream for more! Shhhh!

Lorna Coates (11)
Cawley Lane JIN School

ROSES

Starting from a bud
the roses grow,
as a beautiful flower appears,
a pretty rose waves at me
and says
roses are red
sugar is sweet
and so am I.
A nice scent is in the air.

Halimah Nazir (10)
Cawley Lane JIN School

LOVE POEM

O; I shall not care no more
Even though you are the love of my life
I don't want you here anymore
I don't want you as my wife

The tears trickled down her face
As her husband looked in grace
He returned to his elegant castle
With tears trickling down his face

I shall go now, you will never see me again
You can go with them for all I care
I am moving away
And you will never find me anywhere

You may live here, you may live here not,
You are not my wedded wife
No more, I don't care
You may spoil your life

Steven Alderson (10) & Nathan McCann
Cawley Lane JIN School

THE TIGER

Tiger, tiger prowling round,
Always hunting on the ground.
Jumping down from a tree,
As he gets a sting from a bee.

Tigers purr as soft as silk,
As his cub has mother's milk.
As the tiger cubs settle down,
Daddy tiger goes prowling round.

Tiger's teeth are sharp as a pin,
Yesterday he had some meat from a bin.
Teeth as white as snow,
But are they, I don't know?

Jade Mackay (9)
Cawley Lane JIN School

THE LADYBIRD

Ladybird, ladybird
You are so sweet
Ladybird, ladybird
I want to give you a treat.

Ladybird, ladybird
You shine like the sun
Ladybird, ladybird
You have so much fun.

Ladybird, ladybird
You are like the moon
Ladybird, ladybird
Don't go home so soon.

Ladybird, ladybird
I like your little dots
Ladybird, ladybird
You have black spots.

Ladybird, ladybird
Don't make me cry
Ladybird, ladybird
Don't let me say bye-bye.

Bye-bye.

Nabeela Shahzad & Mevish Jamil (10)
Cawley Lane JIN School

CHRISTMAS TIME

Christmas is a very cold time,
With lots of wintry weather,
It's not very nice for the sun doesn't shine
And it could be much better.

The stars in the sky are very high
And twinkle really bright,
They come out real often, they're sure not shy
And sparkle in the night.

The Christmas trees are really green
And decorated well,
Ours is the nicest I've ever seen,
With tinsel, baubles and bells.

People singing Christmas carols,
Walk up and knock on your door,
You eat your dessert along with swiss rolls
And have more fun than ever before.

The snow outside is cold and damp,
But fun to throw around,
You can laugh and sing and run and jump
And make a lot of sound.

Tamsin Rounding (10)
Cawley Lane JIN School

COLOURS OF THE TIGER AND THINGS HE DOES

The colour of the tiger is bright,
When he's in the long grass he's out of sight.

When he sees something moving in the grass,
He jumps and makes a long pass.

As the sunlight disappears,
The tiger reappears.

When the moonlight is bright,
He starts a big fight.

Kirsty Beverley (10)
Cawley Lane JIN School

THE FEAR ZONE

Signs of trouble
Going with a big *bang*

Second man shot in city
Face of gun murder victim
Man killed, two are injured in gang attack
Living in the shadow of fear

Attack on the pension plan
But victim hunt goes on
Just ignore Saint Switch
Crash driver escapes from jail
Man in wall death is fall
School's out for the last time

Dig deep at Oakwell Hall
We must act now
Hunt on for stolen puppies
Sniffing deaths are still falling
Victory for animal protesters
Men are top dogs yet again.

Alex Swithenbank & Michael Dawson (10)
Cawley Lane JIN School

FIREWORKS

Fireworks zooming like rockets
into the midnight sky.
Leaving blazing, colourful trails.
Catherine wheel twirling on the garden fence,
spraying showers of glitter.
Amber flames flickering
and leaping on the fire.
Wood burning Guy Fawkes.
Crackling flames blaze on the bonfire.
Screeching fireworks finally reach the sky
and explode into multicoloured sparkles.
Silvery grey smoke floats calmly
into the darkness,
filling the night air.

Laviza Nisa-Ali (10), Kal Bolas, Samantha Coates &
Nabeel Hussain (11) & Todd Walker (9)
Cawley Lane JIN School

COOL

To be cool, you don't have to follow the rules,
To be cool you have to be funny with loads of money,
To be cool you have to act like a dummy
And that's really funny!

Oh yeah
To be cool.

Ola Jegede (9)
Cawley Lane JIN School

THE BALLAD OF ERIC

Eric was walking home from school
Feeling great and looking cool
His brand new clothes had been designed
By a young, young writer with a great style in mind

But he didn't realise his clothes had been made
For smaller girls, not boys I'm afraid
He was walking home in purple and pink
Which made passers-by look and think

In the same clothes he went to a dance
Where by look or even chance people seemed to like the trend
To them it seemed to really blend

Eric danced, sang and messed about
He ran and talked and did he shout
No one stopped to stare or blink
In fact the next day everyone was in pink!

Ryan Oates (9)
Cawley Lane JIN School

MY HEADTEACHER

He's a broken chair
An owl looking for his prey
A puma staring eagle-eyed
He's a baby crying when he's just got out of bed
He's a daffodil in the summer.

Lee Hughes (10)
Cawley Lane JIN School

Spring Poetry

A spring day is like a cheerful world
The rain falls like a shower
The sun shines like a yellow planet
The sky resembles a sheet of blue paper
Baby chickens glow like amber lights
Spring lambs look like white fluffy clouds
A spring day is like a cheerful world
Flowers shoot from the ground like fireworks
Blossom floats like icebergs
Spring breathes like a new world.

Jack Walshaw (11)
Cawley Lane JIN School

Firework Display

Whiz, crackle, pop, bang went the fireworks
As the bonfire glittered and sparkled in the darkness.
As the flames danced in the midnight sky,
Licking the darkness.
Morning appears and the bonfire lays smouldering,
Silvery, hot, sparkling ashes.
Cold and empty fireworks,
Asleep on the ground,
For another year.

Samuel Strand (11)
Cawley Lane JIN School

MY HEADTEACHER

He is a bouncy chair
A cunning fox watching his prey
The king of the castle
A livid barking dog
A glum morning and a
Cheerful afternoon.

Jade Walker & Leanne Brown (10)
Cawley Lane JIN School

THE SPOOKY SKELETON

The spooky skeleton was in the house,
He was as quiet as a mouse.
Then creaking, rattling noises I heard,
Coming from the living room.
Then I heard rattling noises coming from upstairs.
I kept on saying to myself, 'It's only a dream,
It's only a dream'
Thinking that it might work,
But I had to try something else.
Then I managed to go to sleep,
Then I woke up, the skeleton had gone,
I was so happy,
But was I?
Would I see it again?

Greta Wilding (9)
Colden Primary School

SKELETONS

Skeletons are scary,
Skeletons are white,
Skeletons are spooky,
Skeletons like night,
Skeletons are funny,
Skeletons are big,
Skeletons have clothes,
But skeletons like tig,
We are all scared of skeletons,
But they just hide and laugh,
Skeletons don't like hot things,
Like a warm bath.

Benjamin John Page (9)
Colden Primary School

RATTLING

R attling bones you hear at night, ooooh ooooh
A t night you get a fright because the skeleton is looking in
T ap, tap, it is running and there is nobody there
T o the skeleton we go and we shout, 'Come out, we're not afraid'
L ike a whizz he comes out and he was scared but we killed him
   (we're the champions, yes, yes, yes)
I n the night we're not afraid
N othing scares us now he's gone
G oing to wake up in morning and nothing will be there.

Ashleigh Louise Tunnicliffe (7)
Colden Primary School

SKELETONS

Skeletons are spooky
Skeletons are spiky
Skeletons are strong
Skeletons are slimy
Skeletons are slippery
Skeletons are scary
Skeletons are silent
Skeletons are skinny
Skeletons are stiff
Skeletons are secret
Skeletons are solid
And skeletons are special.

Isabelle McCart (8)
Colden Primary School

SPOOKS

D irty graveyard by the church,
I t is mysterious and dark,
R ibs are rattling on a dark night,
T wo big skeletons walking down a road,
Y ou will not come to the church,

B ig, brown skeletons in a graveyard,
O nly scared people are scared
N aughty skeletons on the road
E veryone is dying in the town
S melly flesh of dead people.

George William Emsley (8)
Colden Primary School

SKELETON

Skeletons are spooky, hard and rough
Why is everybody scared of skeletons?
I don't believe in skeletons
Skeletons roaring in the woods, seeing how to
Stamp down the road,
Now it is night-time.

Andrea Anderson (8)
Colden Primary School

THE SKELETONS

The graveyard is silent at night
Until the skeletons start to fight.
Rattling bones, a terrible sight,
The people phone the nearest police
And they arrested the local priest.
They said he should keep his church in control at night,
I do until the skeletons come out to fright.

Lucy Kelly (8)
Colden Primary School

SKELETON

You need a skeleton
Because if you didn't have
A skeleton you would not be able to walk
But if you did have a skeleton
You wouldn't walk.

Jake Jackson (7)
Colden Primary School

The Skeleton

The skeleton was in my house
He was being as quiet as a mouse
Everything he did he made a noise
I tried to look at my toys
But my eyes were fixed to the skeleton
He had his butcher's knife ready for the kill
I hope he doesn't kill me, I'm ill
His teeth all yellow and rotten
Then with a cackle he disappears
Rattling up the stairs
There was another skeleton, they were in pairs
They were coming to me, I'm in for it now
I tried to shout
But they covered my mouth
Then I heard a scream
It was my little sister, Hannah
The other one had got her
I kicked the skeleton
I got him down
His butcher's knife on the ground
'You defeated me' the skeleton said
The other one fell down dead.

Taryn Chantal Rath (9)
Colden Primary School

The Skeleton Is Coming

Here comes the skeleton, clanking its bones,
Here comes the skeleton, clanking and swirling his head,
Two-legged skeleton hopping about,
Its cheesy smile just freaks you out
Remember, beware of the skeleton!

Zoe Cox (7)
Colden Primary School

SKELETON

S trange, mysterious night, spook staring at you
K eeping very still, waiting for the kill
E nter at your doom, the atmosphere gets tense
L ive or die, the skeleton is here
E nter at your peril, the skeleton is here
T o the door you run, echoes everywhere, die, die
O h you run, run, hear a voice say, die, die, die
N o one knows, suddenly you see it pelting towards you,
Die, die, die, the museum trembles with its echoes.

Sean Luke Smithies (7)
Colden Primary School

SPOOK

S pooky skeleton on the street
K icking and crying, elephant bones everywhere
E erie skeletons stamping down the road
L iving skeletons getting out of their graves
E erie bones dancing everywhere
T oothless skeletons eating everybody
O h no, they're looking for me
N o, I can't die.

Louis Haigh (7)
Colden Primary School

FUNNY BONES

F unny bones are funny
U nder the floor, the floorboards creak
N ow hear the skull laugh and laugh
N ever hit your funny bone or
Y our elbow will hurt

B ones are really important things
O n the floor your feet stand
N ear the dark corner is a mystery bone
E very night, every day you use your bones in every way
S o use your bones carefully, you don't want to lose them, do you?

Elizabeth Lamle (8)
Colden Primary School

RETURN OF THE SKELETON

The skeleton comes from his grave
Shadows made by the moonlight
A shining sword in his hand
Blood dripping from his bones
From the grave
The skeleton is back
Still wearing his pirate hat.

Andrew Lyons (9)
Colden Primary School

SKELETONS

S pooky skeletons all around,
K illing others as they bound,
E verything's bones,
L ight shining through the bones,
E choes heard, then the rough fight,
T oothless skeletons down at the pub,
O n their way for alcohol,
N aughty skeletons scaring you,
S cary skeletons on the ground.

Daniel Edward McCormack (8)
Colden Primary School

RATTLING

R attling along the skeleton goes,
A terrible sight he is,
T errible with his broken nose,
T rudge, trudge, trudge, until he gets in a tiz,
L oads of people running away, screaming,
I n the half light
N obody's here because they're all shouting
'G o away from him,
    Otherwise he'll give you a fright!'

Lizzie Johnes (8)
Colden Primary School

SKELETON

S pooky skeleton saw some salmon
K illed the skeleton in the spooky night
E very night the skull goes walking in the dark
L ight and a few flashes and snap
E verybody knows the rib and the brain walk
T o the shadow to the left lives a skeleton
O nce there lived a skeleton, spooky
N o skeleton in the spooky night.

Joshua Crawshaw (7)
Colden Primary School

THE SKELETON'S NIGHT OUT

S pooky skeleton saw some salmon
K icking and crying
E lephant bones everywhere
L eaping leopard bones, jumping jaguars
E mpty eye sockets
T oothless skulls staring at me
O n to the streets the skeletons lurk for prey
N owhere to be seen, it kills its prey.

Jocob Clayton (7)
Colden Primary School

THE SKELETONS

Beware, beware, the skeletons are here
They're scratching and hissing like bears
Hiss they go, hiss
They slither through the hallway
They creak up the stairs
Into your room
Eyes like flames
In the morning
What a shame they're not here.

Alexander Kay (9)
Colden Primary School

MR WINTER!

Winter comes to devour the autumn cool,
slyly snatching the last sound of nature.
It spits out icy flakes of everlasting leftovers,
covering the crispy, rustling colours.
It lays a pool of frozen water over the land,
blotting all of the planet.
It fires out a smoky layer of air,
camouflaging all of the houses.
It brawls out all traces of heat,
losing no battles or strength.
It blocks out ounces of light,
plotting the world into darkness!

Jonathan Paul Crossley (11)
Field Lane Primary School

WINTER

Winter gnaws through the autumn coolness,
slyly swallowing the last sounds of nature.
It spits out icy flakes of temporary leftovers,
covering the crispy, rustling colours.

Crawling over everything autumn left behind,
disappearing, imperceptible to the naked eye.
Slithering over the carpet of autumn,
leaving just white, like a cartoon scene disappearing.

It stretches over a ground of leaves
banishing the grass.
It hovers in the autumn air,
icy cold and stinging.

Richard Strauss (10)
Field Lane Primary School

THE BEGINNING OF NATURE

Winter gnaws through the autumn cool,
slyly swallowing up the last sounds of nature.
It spits out icy flakes of everlasting leftovers,
covering the crispy, rustling carpet of colours.
Carefully, it places a blanket of white feathers,
like tears of diamonds of a tiny child in Heaven.
The last fragment of glass taken from the floor,
thrown away into the refuse of seasons.
It is a skilled spy plotting and planning,
quickly rushing away from the slippery hands of trouble.
Winter holds all the world in its cold hands,
just like two love birds snuggling their young.

Natasha Louise Hrab (11)
Field Lane Primary School

WINTER

Winter gnaws through the autumn cool,
slyly swallowing up the last sounds of nature.
It spits out icy flakes of everlasting leftovers,
covering the crispy, rustling carpet of colours.

It slithers through the darkness of the ground,
rumbling past the dull brown trees.
Slowly it pounces over the smooth trees,
daring, it freezes the ground.

It drowns the wet, long bushes,
Filling up the grey water's edge,
It races down the slippery stream,
Gliding down the winter's midnight sky.

Cally Scrimshaw (10)
Field Lane Primary School

TRANQUIL SUN

The sun was slowly dripping down,
The beautiful horizon was appearing,
Calm, silent streets, no people around.
The gold horizon was sinking and blending in
The background of the view.
The gold sun was exhausted.
It was like a treasure you have always wanted.
This evening was beautiful.
The gold sun you could have forever.
The tranquil sun was gorgeous.
It shone through windows like a pearl.

Stacey Pease (10)
Henry Moore Junior School

SPRING IS GROWING SO BEAUTIFULLY!

S pring is growing into such
P retty, delicate things!
R ich and beautifully
I n every little way,
N ice is not the word but
G orgeous, such beautiful things that I can't describe them!

I s there anything else that you would want to see?
S ee the buds opening into a beautiful flower, it smells so delightful!

G rowing? Yes they are,
R eally, every single second, nature is doing something important.
O pening up,
W anting to grow
I nto a pretty little flower!
N ow have you seen anything more
G orgeous than this?

S o take a look
O utside, once in a while

B efore you know it,
E verything you see might be beautiful
A nd maybe not just nature but
U s as well!
T ake a look at the people
I n your life and those that are strangers!
F or you see the
U niverse is full of people that
L ive and have a beauty inside their
L ife and
Y et, some people just don't see it!

Jennifer Lee (10)
Henry Moore Junior School

SUNSHINE

The orange sun's sinking
While falling asleep she's blinking
A ball of light descending down
Smiling like a golden clown
She's a round melon
Or a big lemon
She's shining through the golden trees
While blowing in the still, calm breeze
Silent and still she yawns
Ready to get up at dawn
She's setting in the sky
Time for her to say goodbye.

Lauren Betteridge (11)
Henry Moore Junior School

SUNSET

The shadows seemed to dance,
Their ebony figures swallowing all light,
They are people of the moon,
From times of old,
When the world was in shadow.

Now they dance back every day at sunset,
Trying to suck all the light and joy from
The soul of the Earth,
But they never succeed,
For the sky becomes ablaze,
Melting them down into one great
Pool of darkness,
Which covers the world at night.

Laura Feeney (10)
Henry Moore Junior School

The Sunset

In the day, the sun is motionless
So still, so calm
The end of the day draws near
Slowly it subsides
Leaving a gold rainbow in its path
Slowly it closes its eyes
And disappears

The buildings start to rust
Starting to crumble
Like a house shattering into a thousand pieces
People turning into shadows
The town, all hushed, not a sound
The town shutting down
To reset in the morning.

Emma Kelleher (10)
Henry Moore Junior School

The Beach

The sand was as crispy as freshly-made toast
And the twirly home of the hermit crab lay forgotten on the coast.
As I look out I see a blue blanket of icing
And suddenly blue horses with white manes and tails
Come galloping towards the shore;
But turn to nothing but soap beneath my feet.
But the cry of the bird that flies across the sea,
Finally softens,
As the sun on the horizon says goodbye for another day.

Ellen McIntyre (10)
Henry Moore Junior School

Rain

The rain fell quickly, bouncing when hitting the floor.
Endlessly it poured faster every second of every minute.
It lashed against the pavement, splashing everywhere.

Splashing the roofs, everything was dull, miserable and dark
Dim and gloomy all day long.

Drains gushing with water like a gigantic waterfall.
Soggy packets floating along like ships in the sea, like ships in the sea.

People hurrying to get home, umbrellas blowing inside out.
Getting drenched inside and out.
Splishing, splashing, sploshing all the way home again!

Reflections of shops, cars and street lights glimmer and glisten
On the puddles from the heavy rain.

Would you like to be there?

Georgina Knell (11)
Henry Moore Junior School

Companionship

Companionship is as bright as a springtime flower
Companionship tastes like your favourite food
Companionship sounds like a blue jay calling for his mate
Calling . . . calling . . . calling
Companionship feels as soft as a newborn lamb
Companionship lives only in the heart.

Helen Peake (10)
Henry Moore Junior School

Rain

The rain, so hard and misty
Hits at my window panes
It goes down the drains so fast
Like a hard ball
Its misty and foggy look as it falls from the sky

Its individual shapes
Misty-looking
Drops from the dark sky
Thunder appears in the sky
A loud rumbling noise

The rain keeps on pouring
From the sky
Its big raindrops falling
Out of the big, dark-blue sky.

Jessica Evans (10)
Henry Moore Junior School

Chocolate

Chocolate is so yummy for my tummy,
I can gulp it up in one.
When you feel very hungry
And your belly starts to rumble,
Just say these little words
As you clap your hands,
Alakazam touch your hands!

Abbey Winfield (10)
Henry Moore Junior School

SCHOOL WORK

First lesson, *maths!*
Hate it.

Assembly time!
Information time.

Break time!
Chill out.

Second lesson, *English!*
Guess it's OK.

Dinner time!
Eat dinner, yum yum.

Third lesson, *IT!*
Surf, surf, surf!

Break time!
Chill out.

Last lesson, *history!*
Very educational.

The thing is, if you want a good job you need a good education!

**Carly Greatbatch (11)
Henry Moore Junior School**

SHADOWS

The meadowy shadows sneak ahead,
Like the mist in a sleepy bed
Creeping near to the grass themselves
Are the sleepy meadowy shadows.

I watch the misty clouds go by,
As they rumble their way through the sky,
The clouds themselves are dark and dull,
The sky so drowsy, so still and full.

Sasha Timson (11)
Henry Moore Junior School

THE RIVER

Look at the river,
A mysterious, gloomy, monster,
Deep as the ocean,
It swiftly twists and turns.

Listen to the river,
A gurgling, humming baby,
Bubbling like a kettle,
It flows down its path.

Touch the river,
A bumpy, lumpy liquid,
Tickling like a feather,
Moving very swiftly.

Smell the river,
A breath of fresh air,
Frothing like a can of lager,
Leading to the sea.

Drink the river water,
Gulp it down your throat,
Running like a waterfall,
As it flows off the cliff.

Amy Westerman (9)
Henry Moore Junior School

School Subjects

Maths is a subject which I dislike,
I would rather be poked with a red-hot spike.
English is a subject which I don't mind,
That's only if the teacher is being nice and kind.
Art is a subject which I think is good,
But only if we are drawing what I think we should.
Geography is a subject which I think is worse,
So instead of working, I fiddle in my purse.
Science is a subject which I can't stand,
I prefer to draw funny faces on my hand.
Writing poems is what I like best,
Because I can do this better than the rest.

Laura Cartwright (11)
Henry Moore Junior School

Death

Death is as black as a tomb,
It smells like decaying bones,
Death tastes like raw meat,
It sounds like mist,
It feels as sharp as a dagger,
Death lives in the dark of night
Looking for victims.

Bradley West Slater (10)
Henry Moore Junior School

SNOW AND ICE

I can harden myself into ice,
For children to skate on; it feels very nice,
I can soften myself for young children to throw,
Come on and have a go,
Now make a person out of me.

Add a hat, add a scarf,
If you do, I'll be your friend,
Please don't make me come to an end,
Also remember to wrap up warm 'cause I am cold
And never say you haven't been told.

Emma-Louise Leeming (11)
Henry Moore Junior School

THE MONKEY

I can swing from tall trees,
Then land upon my hands and knees,
I am really funky
And I'm extremely jumpy.
I like to eat loads of bananas,
Then put their skins down my best mate's 'jamas,
Before I go to bed I like to pull funny faces,
But then I nearly forget to say my graces.

Stacey-Louise Scott (10)
Henry Moore Junior School

WAR

War is grey, it smells like sweaty socks
It tastes like mouldy potatoes
It sounds horrifying and feels like smashed glass
It lives in the heart of a warrior.

Laurie Kennedy (10)
Henry Moore Junior School

DEATH

Death is the colour of blood-thirsty red
It smells like dead, decaying bodies
Death tastes chewy and gooey, just like slime
It sounds like guns banging
It feels slimy and squashy like mud
And water mixed together
Death lives in *Hell*.

Gemma Louise Scales (9)
Henry Moore Junior School

FEAR

Fear is a dull, dark, patchy grey,
It smells like melting metal,
It tastes hot and spicy
And sounds like thunder,
It lives inside a kettle.

Jemma Fretwell (10)
Henry Moore Junior School

GOLD

The sun is like a tired eye,
Slowly, softly it sinks to the ground.
Trees and people turn to golden trinkets
As quickly as a panther.

A house in the forest is as gold as could be,
A sunset in the wild is a beautiful sight to see.
The horizon like a gem, as valuable as can be,
Oh what a pretty sight for the birds, trees and me.
The sunset is going now and the only things I can see
Are the moon, stars and me.

Martin Duffy (10)
Henry Moore Junior School

SHIMMERING SKY

Slowly the sun is setting
Closing his eyes to sleep
Everything is so quiet, so still
Sinking softly into the tranquil, dark sky
Drowsily it yawns, falling to sleep
The gold moon is shimmering
Shaped like a gold rainbow
Everything is peaceful
So silent, so calm.

Sarah Dyson (10)
Henry Moore Junior School

For Dinner I Had...

For dinner I had a little boy, he tasted rather funny
I think it was because his nose was rather runny

For dinner I had a little baby, she tasted rather chewy
I think it was because her nappy was rather pooey

I didn't taste Gran and Grandad
I think they'll taste rather sour
I wonder what I'll have tomorrow
In the dinner hour?

Eden Spedding (11)
Henry Moore Junior School

Window

There once was a very small window
in a very small room.
An alien looked through the window
and saw different people.
A robot looked through the window
and saw a black ocean of oil.
A boy looked through the window
and saw a land of chocolates.
A ghost looked through the window
and saw life.
The sea crashed through the window
and shattered it.

Scott Jessop (9)
Lady Lane Park School

ELIZABETH

Elizabeth is my cousin, her age is seventeen
I call her Lizzy
She always is so busy
Busy like a bee
'Are you alright?' 'Yes, I'm fine' she says
As she flies round the house in her holey black socks,
T-shirt and jeans
Orange straight hair, always in a bobble
She cuddles me when I'm feeling down
She always likes to play around.

Elizabeth is my cousin, her age is seventeen
Everyone calls her Lizzy
She always is so busy
Busy like a bee
She used to be quite small
But now she's six foot tall.

Rachel Lloyd (8)
Lady Lane Park School

DAD

My dad is tall
With hair that curls
He wears Wallace and Gromit slippers
Whilst whistling and singing as loud as he can.
My dad works hard
Comes home late
But always
Kisses me goodnight.

Daniel Taylor (8)
Lady Lane Park School

OWL

Big, round eyes
Shimmering like a torch
Shiny leaf-shaped feathers
Soft like velvet
Talons sharp and strong
As sharp as meat hooks
Large, powerful wings
Like a graceful aeroplane
Curved hard beak
As tough as stone
Long, strong legs
Straight, like a ruler
Face, staring,
Frightening,
Menacing
Like a wild cat.

Stuart Slingsby (8)
Lady Lane Park School

THE WILD, WILD WEST

The cruel blazing sun,
Forsaken prairie,
Infertile sweltering ground,
Dangerous airless land,
The wild, wild west.

The cold, bitter air,
Unsafe darkness,
Terrifying silence,
The horse treading ground,
The howling coyote,
The wild, wild west.

Parched, scorching air,
No sound,
Everything is silent,
Just the smoky crackling fire,
Rich, red explosions,
The wild, wild west.

Oliver O'Leary (11)
Lady Lane Park School

THE MAKING OF A PICTURE

To make a picture, sit on a lawn
And cut a slice of a child's laugh.
Put it under a book of happy thoughts
To push out the noise,
This will be your paper.

To make a picture, you need a brush,
Take a feather from an exotic bird,
Or a flame from a burning fire,
These will be your tools.

To make a picture, you also need paint,
For silver take a strand of a spider's web
And for black take the spider.
For red gather the morning sky
And for gold take the sun.

To paint a picture, go back in time
And grab the few last moments of someone's life,
Paint over to give a 3D and scary effect.
This time go into the future and bring back a
Fabulous new mind-blowing thing,
This will be your picture.

Lottie McDowell (10)
Lady Lane Park School

THE GOLDFISH

It's a boring life being a goldfish,
going up and down,
up and down
and when it's feeding time,
well, yum! Yum!

But it's a boring life being a goldfish,
good job I wasn't one!
I mean a goldfish (boring life!)

Amesh Ahir (9)
Lady Lane Park School

THE MYSTICAL SUITCASE

I will add to my suitcase
A football that bounces and scores
A goal post shattering under a powerful shot
A goal keeper's glove blocking a save
I will add to my suitcase
Chocolate and drinks
Flowers dropping from the sky
And rain coming from the floor
I will have a sheet of Blue John stone to remind me of the cave
And onyx on the outside.

Joseph Hathaway (10)
Lydgate J&I School

My Swirly Bin

I will throw in my bin
an old dusty lion skin
that is torn and battered.
An old piece of china
found from underground.
And a doll
with one eye.

I will throw in my bin
a poor tiger
that lost its teeth.
A toy that squeals
that's lost its squeaker.
A trail of feathers
fallen from a snow-coloured dove.

I will throw in my bin
a chair with three legs
that wobbles about.
A skeleton
that's lost its funny-bone.
And the lead of a pencil
that's been chewed to shreds.

My bin swirls like the
waves of the sea.
With boats on the side
shining with glee.
When you hit the lid
it swings back and forth
as smoothly as a swing.

Adam Webster (11) & Jason Stott (10)
Lydgate J&I School

I Will Put In My Suitcase

I will put in my suitcase
A yellow star that glows in the dark,
Some sun cream so my body doesn't burn,
My favourite football I should play with.

I will put in my suitcase
My swimming kit to swim in the Antarctic,
A hat to keep me cool on the beach,
Some blue sunglasses to make me look at the sun.

I will put in my suitcase
A blanket and towel to keep me warm and dry,
My bucket and spade to play in the sand,
Some shorts and T-shirts to keep me cool.

I shall surf in my suitcase
The metal of an old-fashioned sewing machine,
Some locks to keep it safe,
All the memories of our trips,
The pictures of all the places we have visited.

Elmedin Kadiric & Shakil Ahmed (11)
Lydgate J&I School

My Magic Box

I shall trap in my box
The singing from a feathery bird,
The buzz from a busy honey-making bee
And the loudest storm in the sky.

I shall trap in my box
The first word from a baby,
The grin of a cat
And the loudest bang there has ever been.

My box is fashioned from silver, diamonds and pearls,
With glitter on the lid and whispers in the corner,
Its hinges are made from elephant tusks and
Horns from a rhinoceros.

I will swim in my box,
With the wet and shiny dolphins,
That live in the sea,
Then they will swim away, leaving me,
While I watch them go.

Stacie Gelder (10)
Lydgate J&I School

My Magic Box

I will put in my box
The fastest leopard from Africa speeding around,
The slowest turtle from the Caribbean swimming calmly by
And a skipping kangaroo with a mind of its own.

I will put in my box
A model of a car as stiff as a rock,
A picture on a wall hung proudly,
The whistling of the wind whistling through my face.

I will put in my box
A plane gliding through the air,
An alien spacecraft orbiting the Earth at millions of miles per hour,
A submarine swirling through the water.

My box is made from shiny copper
And the hinges made from a dragon's toe bones,
The shiniest shells printed on it from all around the world.

Ben Helliwell & Dale Smylie (10)
Lydgate J&I School

I Will Put In My Box

I will put in my box
Sun cream so it reminds me of the Sahara,
Some floppy slippers to surf the ocean floor,
Swimming kit to surf the Atlantic.

I will put in my box
Sun glasses to keep the sun away,
The hot golden sand,
The swish of the Atlantic Ocean.

I will put in my box
A blanket to keep me warm,
A pillow as soft as a baby's bum.

I will surf the Atlantic Ocean with my flippers,
Way down to the ocean floor.
I shall surf in my box
It's made out of the softest leather with secrets inside,
The middle is my belongings
And that's my secret box.

Adam Kotia (11)
Lydgate J&I School

My Box

I will put in my box
A stunt bike with a mind of its own,
A scooter that flies.
I will put in my box
A skunk that stinks like a dustbin,
A baboon that breaks wind a thousand times.

I will put in my box
A very fierce lion from Indian,
A kangaroo from Australia
And a monkey from Mozambique.

My box
It is made of the shiniest gold,
With shells from every corner of the world,
The hinges are made of marble which squeak
Every time you open it.

Judd Ledgard (11) & Mark Flynn (10)
Lydgate J&I School

SKY

The sky is a large blue blanket
covering the world
During the day the light
shines through it

The clouds are the parts
of the blanket that's fallen out
When the clouds move it is like
someone shaking the blanket to clean it

When the light fades away
and the day has gone
There is darkness all night long
except the glow of the stars and moon

When it rains, the clouds are mucky
so someone cleans them
And the water comes down
to make rain

When it thunders, it's someone
playing tug of war with the clouds
The loud bang is someone
having a pillow fight.

Becky Barham (11)
Lydgate J&I School

COMPUTER

I will insert into my computer

A sunken ship old and rusty,
An aeroplane with no survivors,
A car that's speeding on the motorway.

I will insert into my computer

A fly flying into the World Wide Web,
A rabbit digging into the Earth's core,
A deadly shark swimming towards his prey.

I will insert into my computer

A person who sees dead people,
A man who has been inserted into the Matrix,
A woman using Jackie Chan's deadly stunts.

I will insert into my computer

People cringing and shivering watching the Blackpool roller coaster
Down the track,
The horror on people's faces as they ride the ghost train,
The despair of the war-ridden countries.

My computer is fashioned from lovely shining glass that will
Catch the human eye,
The sparkling wires melt the exterior plastic,
The edges have an aerial signalling to outer space.

I will insert myself into my computer and explore the infinite Internet,
I will wash ashore the hardrive and I will become unplugged.

Marcus Horsley (11) & Nathan Wilkinson (10)
Lydgate J&I School

CHESTNUT

Chestnut you are a shiny star in the sparkling sky
In the moonlight shining like glitter
Hard and prickly

Children reach me and pull me!
So I am so high, hidden by the leaves,
Birds and squirrels don't see me hidden.

Hard as a door, secret inside,
High in the tree tumbling down!
With leaves all over the place.

Smash! It falls down on the grass,
Till autumn.

Syka Kouser (9)
Ravensthorpe CE Junior School

WINTERTIME

Wintertime is a time for snow,
There are lots of places where you can go,
There is a robin on the bird table,
There is a squirrel running into the stable,
There's a snowman built on my street
And it's melting now because of the sun's heat,
All the rivers are frozen solid,
I cannot stop sneezing, I feel horrid,
It doesn't matter, it's nearly spring,
There's going to be lots of birds
Who can dance and sing.

Kristian Nicholson (10)
Ravensthorpe CE Junior School

WINTER!

Happy New Year
Santa's here
Wrapped up warm
Ready for the storm

Riding on the sledge
Start off at the edge
Snow is cold
The old man walks bold

Children wish
For a sweetie dish
Mum says 'Where's your fleece?
And pick up your niece.'

Cold and frost
There's something you've lost
I wear my gloves
Winter's one of my loves.

Sonia Hussain (10)
Ravensthorpe CE Junior School

ODE TO A SHINY CONKER

Conker!
You are as shiny as a star
A ball of polished wood
You will fall off when you are ready
Like a falling gem
Lots of children come for you
You will be pleased to be their treasure
Oh lovely, lovely conker.

Noshaba Butt (9)
Ravensthorpe CE Junior School

PETS, PETS, PETS

Pets, I wonder what they eat?
Meat feet?
I wonder do cats eat dog food?
Do dogs eat cat food?
I just don't know.
Do dogs live in ponds?
Do ducks live in kennels?
I'm not quite sure.
Do hamsters eat fish food?
Do fish eat hamster food?
I think so.
Do you know what size an elephant is?
Size of a mouse, mole or house?
Is a mouse the size of a house
Or a woodlouse?
A parrot rhymes with carrot,
I wonder if it eats it?

Annie Wilcock (8)
Ravensthorpe CE Junior School

ODE TO AN ACORN

Shiny as a glass eye
You stand out amongst the rest
When the wind blows
You gently fall amongst
The green grass in the meadow
With your smooth brown shell
And cup to hold you
What a treasure!

Jeremy Wright (10)
Ravensthorpe CE Junior School

Hands

They can twist and turn like ballerinas,
They push and pull, bring and fetch,
But never seem to stop or sweat.

They pinch and nip and sometimes threaten
And as their fingers meet their pink rosy palms,
They tighten up, scrunch and squeeze,
Maybe to cause a slight harm.

Big hands,
Small hands,
Fat hands,
Thin hands.

They give signals and try to communicate,
They can speak a silent language,
They wiggle. Open and close like doors.
What do you do with yours?

Teresa McGrath (10)
Ravensthorpe CE Junior School

The Ninth Floor

No one ever dares to open the door
To the ninth floor.
There was a girl who went to the ninth floor
And never got to see daylight of day anymore.

Every day at midnight
Her dad wakes up in the ninth floor to see some candlelight,
He follows it silently,
Stares at his daughter's image quietly.

He thinks it is a dream,
Like someone shining a laser beam.
In the elevator there are wails and moans heard,
Like a lonely chirping bird.

Sohail Khan (11)
Ravensthorpe CE Junior School

ANIMALS

What do animals eat?
Some eat carrots
And some eat meat.
Hamsters eat all kinds of things,
But ducks eat bread
And dogs eat meat.
Animals eat everything.

What do cats eat?
Do cats eat bread? Do cats eat meat?
I just don't know!

Monkeys eat bananas,
But mice eat cheese.
Rabbits eat lettuce.
Do gerbils eat peas?
Animals eat everything.

What do frogs eat?
Do they eat flies and bugs?
I just don't know!

Animals eat all kinds of things,
Just like me!

Rebecca Hayward (7)
Ravensthorpe CE Junior School

HANDS

Hands are like worms,
Wiggling all the time,
Scratching like tigers.

Skinny and thin,
Stubby and fat,
Short and long,
Big and small.

Tearing and cutting,
Poking and piking,
Flicking and picking,
Dipping and splashing.

Smacking and punching,
Thumping and bashing,
Banging and slamming,
Holding and dropping!

Francesca Leona Dec (11)
Ravensthorpe CE Junior School

THE BIRD

Swishing, whizzing in the sky
Swirling, streaming through the clouds
Zooming, swinging like a rocket
Falling, swooping toward the ground
And flying over the noisy crowds.

Pecking at seed on the ground,
Splashing in the bird baths,
Singing in early morning,
Skipping down the garden path.

Sam Wilcock (10)
Ravensthorpe CE Junior School

MY HANDS NEVER STOP WORKING

My hands never stop working
I'm surprised they don't wear away
My hands just keep on moving,
Each and every day.

At school they write,
At home they play,
On the PC they click, click, click
And if you're very talented,
You can do a magic trick.

Big hands,
Small hands,
Fat hands,
Thin hands,
We couldn't live without them,
Hands, hands, hands never stop.

Nathan Driver (10)
Ravensthorpe CE Junior School

DANIEL'S POEM FOR LIFE

I love working on my PC
I like watching my TV
I like doing nothing
Except eating my tea

I like sausages
I like peas
I love fried bread
With lots of beans.

Daniel Paul Hemingway (11)
Ravensthorpe CE Junior School

MY PRECIOUS HANDS

My hands help me,
My hands are precious,
My hands don't do their work for a fee,
For they are my precious hands.

They bend, twist and turn,
They look like slim-figured rulers,
Their homework is to know how to communicate
And so they are my precious hands.

Small hands,
Big hands,
Fat hands,
Thin hands,
These are my precious hands.

Neelam Uddin (10)
Ravensthorpe CE Junior School

COCK-A-DOODLE-DO!

Birds are singing, Dad is snoring.
Floorboards are creaking, dogs are barking.
Brother is shaving, Mum is yawning.
Toilet is flushing, clocks are ticking.
Brother arguing, Dad is shouting.
Mum calling, brother laughing.
Family stamping down the stairs.
Mum putting on the kettle, brother watching cartoons.
Water boiling, doors slamming.
Water being poured, brother jumping on the sofa.

Ambreen Hanif (10)
Ravensthorpe CE Junior School

The Sun

The sun was burning,
As the whole world was turning.
It shone like flashes of light,
It was very bright.
It was boiling hot,
For the flowers in a pot.
The ground was steaming,
As the sun was gleaming.
It was like an orange in the sky,
It wanted you to fly high
To say goodbye.

Ishrat Zahoor (10)
Ravensthorpe CE Junior School

The Carrot

The carrot is a magic wand,
Which lives off water from your pond.

It is a hungry orange lion,
Which can run for at least a mile.

It is a sneaky orange snake,
Wrapped around a brownish branch
(From near a lake.)

Until one day it is devoured,
By a hungry human bean!

Christopher Stead (11)
St Anne's RC Primary School, Keighley

WHAT IS A FRIEND?

A friend is someone
who will help you
when you fall.

A friend is a rock,
someone who you can
lean on when you stumble.

A friend is someone
who will keep all
your secrets

And a friend will
expect this off you
too.

Rebecca Lindley (11)
St Anne's RC Primary School, Keighley

THE MOON

The moon is a 10p that has fallen
down the drain from Heaven.
It is a biscuit getting eaten bit by bit every night.
It's a shimmering stone floating in space
with its light reflected by a £1 coin.
Other planets guide their way through this
dark and gloomy world.

Emma Dodd (10)
St Anne's RC Primary School, Keighley

SCHOOL

School is boring,
Keeps me snoring.

Art is fancy,
For a nancy.

Science is smart,
Better than art.

Games are cool,
For a school.

Maths is great,
I can't wait.

English, whoopee!
It's not daily.

End of school, yes,
Better go home I guess.

Andrew Hall (11)
St Anne's RC Primary School, Keighley

THE INTER NET

There once was a thing called the Inter Net
Spiders built it for things that were hard to get
It caught a bug
The system glugged
'Oh dear, oh no! I've crashed! I'm dead!'

Nicholas Smith & Jordan Wise (11)
St Anne's RC Primary School, Keighley

THIS IS A POEM

'This is a poem'
'Oh no it isn't!'
'Oh yes it is!'
'Well, it's certainly not a pantomime'
'Well don't go on about all this, oh no it isn't stuff'
'Let's just agree on what it is. OK?'
'Yes, it's a poem'
'Oh no it isn't'
'You've started again. Fine, what do you think it is?'
'It's a group of words'
'Fine'
'At last we agree'
'This is a poem.'

Thomas Gee (11)
St Anne's RC Primary School, Keighley

CANDY APPLES

A candy apple is a bright red ball,
It is a crunchy carrot,
It is an irregular sphere with a toffee coat on,
It can have many toppings,
Chocolate,
Toffee,
Caramel,
100s and 1000s!
Or maybe
Chocolate sprinkles.
It is a frosty morning with a warm sun.

Lucy Brown (10)
St Anne's RC Primary School, Keighley

CHOCOLATE

Milk chocolate is a flat rugby ball
White chocolate is a fresh clean sheet
Orange chocolate is the sun
Pink chocolates are your lips
Dark chocolate is the blackboard
All chocolate is yum!

Tamara Patti (10)
St Anne's RC Primary School, Keighley

THE SKY

A velvet sheet that is the sky,
The clouds are ice creams floating up high.
A golden coin that is the sun,
I love the sky, it's such good fun.

Paul Owens (11)
St Anne's RC Primary School, Keighley

A TARGET

A bowling ball is a lion running swiftly,
It tries to catch as many weak animals as it possibly can!
The pins are very weak animals, they cannot defend themselves,
Unlike a lion.
A lovely target for a hungry, hungry *lion!*

James Gorman (11)
St Anne's RC Primary School, Keighley

NIGHT-TIME

He gallops through the valley deep,
Looking in on children's sleep,
Giving dreams to everyone,
Until the rising of the sun.

He gallops under the midnight sky,
Glittering and gleaming his bright eyes,
Children sleeping safe and sound,
In their beds they can be found.

He gallops round on his last look,
Passing by a running brook,
Waiting for the sun's first peep,
He closes his eyes and goes to sleep.

Laura Wild (11)
St Anne's RC Primary School, Keighley

THE THING IN THE ATTIC

Scratch, scratch. What's in the attic?
Miaow, miaow. Sounds like a monster!
The lock is loose!
Arrrrr maybe a r . . . r . . . rat?
Yeah, I'll get my cat!
Scratch, scratch. There it goes again!
I'm scared, a m . . . m . . . monster?
Hey, the door's opening!
Oh it's my cat with a rat!

Jonathan Taylor (10)
St Anne's RC Primary School, Keighley

THE CHASE

Ben the dog
chased Gem the cat,

Gem the cat
chased Sousa the bird,

Sousa the bird
chased Floppsy the rabbit,

Floppsy the rabbit
chased Scherzi the mouse,

while Scherzi was eating the cheese.

Lauren Bilney, Jenifer Beckett & Claire Rowley (10)
St Anne's RC Primary School, Keighley

MY FRIEND

He's a really cool dude,
His cool colour is green,
His month is January,
His place is Jimmy G's,
His weather is snow,
His clothing is cool sunglasses
And cool pants,
He's a cool climbing frame,
His TV programme is
Three Friend and Jerry.

Josh Fleming (9)
St Anne's RC Primary School, Keighley

The Forest

In a silent, deep forest
There lies a lot of secrets
Of the old willow tree

The old willow tree
Looks like a big
Ice cream cone with
Icicles hanging off
The top

It's a big hotel for wildlife

It's a big home for
Lumberjacks and maidens

It's a death-trap for some.

Grant Briston (10)
St Anne's RC Primary School, Keighley

My Sister

My sister is blue
On a windy day
At her friend's house,
A sunny day,
She is short trousers,
A sofa in the living room,
Her best TV programme is
Buffy the Vampire Slayer,
She eats fish and chips.

Grace Carroll (9)
St Anne's RC Primary School, Keighley

SPIDER IN THE BATH

Aaaarrrrgghhh
There's a spider in the bath
There's a spider in the bath
What should I do Mum?
There's a spider in the bath!

It looks all slimy Mum
It is blacker than a crayon Mum
It is fatter than you Mum
What should I do?

Kill it if you can my love
Or pour on some cold water my love
Call the RSPCA my love
Do whatever you can!

Here comes the RSPCA my love
Open the door my love
'What can I do for you?' he asked
'What can I do?'

There's a spider in the bath
There's a spider in the bath
Scare it away if you can my love
Don't take too long my love
Do whatever you can!

It isn't too much harm my love
Trap it in a jar my love
I'm too busy my love
Do whatever you can!

Sofia (11)
St Anne's RC Primary School, Keighley

What Is... A Star?

A star is God's angel,
That comes out every night,
It comes to watch over us,
And see if we're alright.

A star is a dragonfly,
Spitting its tiny sparks,
It comes to scare the sun away,
Just before dark.

A star is a cannon ball,
Shot up in the sky,
If you look close enough,
You'll see one flying by.

A star is a nest of glow worms,
That come out every night,
It is fun to watch them
Gleam their gleaming light.

Alexandra Marie Batty & Allanah Shaw (10)
St Anne's RC Primary School, Keighley

My Friend

My friend is bright red,
He's a hot Spanish, autumn morning
In a dry Mexican city,
He's a warm morning,
He's a track suit
And is obsessed with his PlayStation,
He's mad on The Simpsons,
He likes his bit of sticky toffee pudding.

Sam Hill (9)
St Anne's RC Primary School, Keighley

WHAT IS... A DOG?

A dog is like a sausage with four legs,
Its tail is wagging like a teacher's finger,
It is a big, soft fur ball,
It's like a detective sniffing for clues,
Its teeth are as sharp as razor blades,
Its eyes are as shiny as diamonds.

Emma Jayne Cantley (10) & Laura Jayne Lambert (11)
St Anne's RC Primary School, Keighley

MY MUM

My mum is sunny
She is a hot summer's day
On a sandy desert island,
She is calm raindrops,
She is a dress or trousers and tidy hair,
She is Coronation Street
And a steaming cup of tea.

David Rhodes (9)
St Anne's RC Primary School, Keighley

WHAT IS... A STAR?

A star is like a five pence piece
Sailing across a muddy stream
It's like a speckle of moon glitzing in the light
A star is like a twinkling diamond
Resting on a finger.

Danilo Rocchio (10)
St Anne's RC Primary School, Keighley

WHAT IS... THE MOON?

The moon is a big round jigsaw puzzle,
that comes out every night,

It was a ball, coloured in by stars.

It is a fluffy ball with cotton wool in it
and dust sprinkled on top.

The moon is a big white football
that someone kicked into the sky.

Or maybe it just appeared one day
out of nowhere.

Jodie Gorman (10)
St Anne's RC Primary School, Keighley

TEDDY BEARS

Some bears are big,
Some bears are small,
Some are cute and cuddly,
Some are little and soft,
Some are big and scary,
Some are toys! Or are they?
Some bears spend the night on your bed,
Dreaming about honey,
Keeps me warm on a windy night.

Jade Charlton (11) & Joshua Payne (10)
St Anne's RC Primary School, Keighley

WHAT IS... THE MOON?

The moon is a white jigsaw puzzle
that comes out at night.

It's a ball cut into a moon shape.

It's a fluffy cloud with cotton wool
with dust on top from the sky.

It's a piece of cloud cut into
the right shape.

It's a ball of cheese.

Katie Hickman (10)
St Anne's RC Primary School, Keighley

MY FRIEND

My friend is the colour of the sunshine
When she smiles,
She is a warm afternoon in summer,
She is in Caritmacross with her grandma, in winter,
because she likes snow,
She is a shady baseball cap
On a sofa sleeping,
The programme my friend is
Is One Foot in the Grave,
She is warm chicken.

Haylie James (9)
St Anne's RC Primary School, Keighley

THE SEA

The sea is a person
Who is calling to me,
The waves are her arms
That are reaching for me.

The gentleness of the horizon
Is the hem of her dress,
The golden beach
Is her long hair.

She calls to me
When I'm alone,
We are friends.

Sarah Marshall (11)
St Anne's RC Primary School, Keighley

MY FRIEND

My best friend is a bright shining sun, yellow
On a warm summer's day,
She is the cinema,
My friend is the brightest star,
She is the softest sofa,
My friend is a lilac T-shirt,
She is Sabrina The Teenage Witch
And a nice piece of broccoli.

Sian Horsman (9)
St Anne's RC Primary School, Keighley

MY SISTERS

My sisters can be summer
but also winter.
They can be orange
but also black.
They can be a bouncy bed
or a chair full of splinters.
They can be sunshine
or a sudden thunderclap,
but whatever happens
they will still be my sisters
to boss me 'cause that's what big sisters do!

Christina Cox (9)
St Anne's RC Primary School, Keighley

A KITTEN CALLED MITTEN

I had a little kitten
And I called it Mitten,
It was so very cosy
And very, very dozy,
It lay on the mat
With my mother's hat,
It had a little nap
And wore a stupid cap,
My mum left a trap
And left the floorboards to flap.

Kirsty Cummins (10)
St Anne's RC Primary School, Keighley

My Friend

My friend is pink,
On a hot summer's day,
As the sun shines so bright.
She is a bright pink dress,
She loves to read,
She also is a mastermind
And loves salad, so cold.

Adriana Gentile (9)
St Anne's RC Primary School, Keighley

My Big Sister

My big sister is *gold,*
She is a bright summer's morning
In a beauty salon,
She is a bright summer's sun
Lording over me
And an untidy desk,
She is a soap fan
And a bar of chocolate.

Charlotte Beaumont (9)
St Anne's RC Primary School, Keighley

A Football Is . . .

A football is like a bird,
flying into the net,
being kicked and whacked by players,
it must be feeling bad.

A football is like a monkey,
rolling and rolling around,
it must be getting dirty,
on Liverpool's muddy ground.

Luciano Fiore (10)
St Anne's RC Primary School, Keighley

MY MUM

My mum is sky blue,
A hot summer's morning
In a small garden,
She is a shining rainbow
In a hot, warm place,
A cosy bed on a cold morning,
She's a soap fanatic
And a plate of shepherd's pie.

Daniel Mulcahy (10)
St Anne's RC Primary School, Keighley

MY DAD

My dad is green,
He is a cold winter morning
In an icy park,
He is rain pattering on the window,
He is trousers and a jacket
And an untidy table,
He is News at Ten
And a tuna sandwich.

Zetoon Zafar (10)
St Anne's RC Primary School, Keighley

My Brother

My brother is dark green,
He is a dull autumn day,
He is a thunderstorm,
He's a dirty rugby kit
And he's a messy bedroom,
He is a wrestler
And a cold Chinese takeaway.

Jordan Hudson (10)
St Anne's RC Primary School, Keighley

The Galaxy Poem

G elatoss is scorching as can be,
A natross is surrounded just by sea,
L onjesset is made of sand,
A ccury is cold enough to freeze your hand,
X enatour is covered with mountains,
Y enjasso is made of fountains.

Jacob Driver (9)
St Anne's RC Primary School, Keighley

My Uncle

My uncle is black,
He's a cold January night
In a hot steamy kitchen
On a cold day,
In a James Bond suit,
He's a PP7 silent gun,
He's a James Bond fanatic,
He's a warm spicy curry.

Luke Hindle (10)
St Anne's RC Primary School, Keighley

VICKY

Vicky is my mate,
She is also great.
She always makes it fun,
So we can get it done.
She loves to watch Popstars,
She loves to climb monkey bars.
She loves Winnie The Pooh
And Tigger too.
So my mate is great!

Amy Louise Harper (9)
St Anne's RC Primary School, Keighley

MY GRANDAD

My grandad is honey orange,
He is a sunny spring,
He loves the bookies,
He likes the sun for gardening,
He wears dull, brown, black clothes,
He loves his cream chair,
He likes football with Leeds United,
He loves his fresh mussels
From the sea.

Aidan Carter (9)
St Anne's RC Primary School, Keighley

My Friend

My friend is fiery red,
She is a warm summer's day
On a shady beach,
She is a bright star on a frosty night,
She is a baggy pair of combats
And a big bouncy bed,
She is 'Popstars' on Wednesday night,
She is a bowl of spicy curry.

Caitlin Schofield (10)
St Anne's RC Primary School, Keighley

My Friend

My friend is sunny yellow,
She is a bright shining rainbow
In a hair salon,
She is a clear blue sky,
She is a track suit,
She is an untidy bedroom,
She is a Tweenie
And a piece of flapjack.

Krystina Murray (9)
St Anne's RC Primary School, Keighley

Armed Forces

A jet fighter is an eagle,
Targeting its prey, ready for the kill.

A tank is a panther,
Lurking in the jungle stealthily on the look-out.

A submarine is a shark,
Lurking in the depths, ready to intercept and destroy.

The infantry are ants,
Ready to fight for their colony.

Jonathan Iwachiw (11)
St Anne's RC Primary School, Keighley

A SMALL MAN

I saw a small man
With a tiny transit van,
His brother died
Because he got fried,
Where did he go?
I don't know!
Did he go to Heaven
Or did he go to Devon?

Jonathan Stead (10)
St Anne's RC Primary School, Keighley

CALLY

C razy and cunning,
A ttempting to do things,
L ikely to stop talking,
L ucky in games,
Y appy when she comes in class.

Victoria Levy (8)
St Chad's CE Primary School, Brighouse

SEAS

S pinning round and round.
E ntertaining.
A mazing.
S alty as can be.

Daniel Wetton (9)
St Chad's CE Primary School, Brighouse

PETS

C harlie, my cute and cuddly cat,
H ow she loves to play,
A nd cause trouble,
R uining Mum's carpets,
L eaping on Grandma's back,
I n her young age she is small, soft,
E ven though her naughtiness gets her into trouble,
   I still love my cat, Charlie.

Jamie Trolland (9)
St Chad's CE Primary School, Brighouse

HORSE

H appy horse,
O ld and alive.
R ainbow-coloured,
S cruffy and spiky as can be,
E legant as well.

Cally Harris (8)
St Chad's CE Primary School, Brighouse

JOSHUA CLARKE

J olly Joshua is as lucky as ever
O bedient as ever
S louching in his chair
H appy and good
U nderstands everything
A s only he could

C heerful and free
L ucky as can be
A head of the rest
R ight through test
K een to do well
E nds with the bell.

Callum Curran (9)
St Chad's CE Primary School, Brighouse

SPIDER

It creeps up the wall
And hangs off the door,
In the moonlit hall
It scuttles to the window.

It looks at the moon,
It wants to go desperately,
Desperately to a blue lagoon,
Where the sun shines brightly.

But it's trapped,
Trapped in the gloomy old castle.

Elliot Fox (9)
St Chad's CE Primary School, Brighouse

UNICORN ISLAND

Unicorn Island is enchanted,
Hot, sunny and finely planted.

The grass is lush, the plants are bright,
It really is a pretty sight.

Graceful dolphins swim in the sea,
They softly squeak to you and me.

The crabs don't nip, the seaweed's not slimy,
The scenery's so great you'll say, 'Core blimey!'

Colourful unicorns gallop in this place,
They gallop so smoothly, they look absolutely ace.

There are fluffy cows from the Highlands,
So come and visit Unicorn Island.

Amy Foulds (9)
St Chad's CE Primary School, Brighouse

THE BIG PIG WHO LOOKED LIKE A TWIG

There once was a pig in the skies
Who always ate 10 foot pork pies
He looked like a spud
And spat out fresh mud
He once killed a swarm of fat bees
He then rudely spat out his food
Which resulted in an unhappy mood
There then was a flood
That sent him flat in the mud
So instead it was mud that he chewed.

Joe Pritchard (9)
St Chad's CE Primary School, Brighouse

PEACE AND QUIET

Peace and quiet, no noise at all,
Not one scream or shout
By children running about,
No crunching when they eat,
Just peace and quiet.
Peace and quiet, no noise at all,
No falling of the pans
By children knocking them down,
No awful laughs by a clown,
Just peace and quiet.
Peace and quiet, no noise at all,
No clattering of toys
By children bashing them together,
At least the noise won't last forever,
Just peace and quiet.
Peace and quiet, no noise at all,
No splashing in puddles,
No humming of cuddles,
No smashing of the windows,
Just peace and quiet.
Peace and quiet, no noise at all,
No smudging of the lipstick,
No splashing in the bath,
No tapping rulers on the table,
Just peace and quiet.
Peace and quiet, no noise at all,
No cracking of the vase,
No shouting in my face,
No tearing of the paper,
Just peace and quiet.

Rachael Ward (8)
St Chad's CE Primary School, Brighouse

SLY SLUG IN LAS VEGAS

Sly slug
Went to Las Vegas
With a snail called Nug.
They went to a gig,
Nug met a big pig,
Yet slug had the greatest of nights
And in the morning,
They both started yawning.
Yet Nug got up
And found a stray pup,
He thought he'd be squashed flat
And that is that,
He never went outside
Again!

Thomas Polotnianka (9)
St Chad's CE Primary School, Brighouse

SAMMY SLUG IN LAS VEGAS

Sammy slug
Went to Las Vegas
With a beetle called Sir Dug.
They went to a casino and won some money
And Sir Dug said, 'That's funny.'
Just then Sammy saw his mummy
And wandered off
And Dug tried to get some money.

Jacob Turner (8)
St Chad's CE Primary School, Brighouse

SAMMY THE SLUG

Sammy the slug
Sat on a mug
Eating a pie
And opened his eye
And saw a fly
That sat on his pie
And said, 'Bye-bye.'

Kristofer Gorringe (8)
St Chad's CE Primary School, Brighouse

RABBIT

Wiggly nose
Never wears bows
Never in a bad mood
Loves its food
And loves to play
All day.

Kate Ratcliffe (9)
St Chad's CE Primary School, Brighouse

PLANET WORLD

There was a planet called Earth,
The aliens thought of its worth,
But when they landed,
They knew they were stranded
And now this was their universe.

Reece Smith (8)
St Chad's CE Primary School, Brighouse

INSECTS IN NEW YORK

The insects are in New York,
Oh no, there's a car, squelch, doh.
Mr Nippy is dead, splatted on the road.
The soldier ants are searching for leftovers,
Maybe they'll have moreovers.
The earwig, Mr Wig has bought a wig,
He's as jolly as a pig.
Sam centipede is doing the hokey-cokey.
Simon slug is slimier than usual
Because of the rubbish,
They're all in New York for the day.

Andrew Halliday (9)
St Chad's CE Primary School, Brighouse

AMY FOULDS

A mazing Amy
M arvellous girl
Y ou'll like her

F or she likes everyone
O range is her favourite colour
U nited Kingdom is where she lives
L ikes dolphins
D ancing like an elephant
S cared as a monkey.

Amy Monday (8)
St Chad's CE Primary School, Brighouse

UNDER THE DEEP BLUE SEA

This is the fish
That got tangled in the seaweed,
That grew in the sea,
Under the deep blue sea.

This is the crab
That saw the fish,
That got tangled in the seaweed,
That grew in the sea
Under the deep blue sea.

This is the shark
That ate the crab,
That saw the fish,
That got tangled in the seaweed,
That grew in the sea
Under the deep blue sea.

This is the electric eel
That electrocuted the shark,
That ate the crab,
That saw the fish,
That got tangled in the seaweed,
That grew in the sea
Under the deep blue sea.

This is the octopus
That fought the electric eel,
That electrocuted the shark,
That ate the crab,
That saw the fish,
That got tangled in the seaweed,
That grew in the sea
Under the deep blue sea.

Ben Bussey (8)
St Chad's CE Primary School, Brighouse

HUGO

H ugo is cute and furry and is
U seful, he scares my fish. He
G oes wherever he wants to
O r he just sleeps!

Richard Mallinson (8)
St Chad's CE Primary School, Brighouse

DOLPHINS

Dolphins swimming gracefully,
Jumping with glee.
Swimming swiftly as can be,
As you might see.
They like to play
In June and May,
But when they say
'You must obey'
Nobody knows what they are saying,
They think that they are just playing.

Olivia Green (9)
St Chad's CE Primary School, Brighouse

FISH

F ish are really boring
I find them when they're snoring
S wimming round and round
H addock fish don't swim on the ground.

Rory Arnold (8)
St Chad's CE Primary School, Brighouse

KITTEN

My best friend
Has a kitten
Which chews my shoes
And plays with a mouse.
It sleeps on the sofa,
It purrs so gracefully
And looks so cute.

Emily Jane Crossley (9)
St Chad's CE Primary School, Brighouse

THE TEACHER FROM HELL

My teacher gives me loads of stick
He makes me work even when I'm sick
He makes up jokes that are not funny
Especially when Hannah brought in a bunny
And even when I'm playing after school
He comes and says to me, 'Remember my rule'
And his rule is to always keep fit
If we don't, we get put in a pit.

Alex Cust (8)
St Chad's CE Primary School, Brighouse

DINOSAURS

Dinosaurs
Do big roars
They eat meat
They have big feet
They eat each other.

Jonathan Lott (8)
St Chad's CE Primary School, Brighouse

THE SCRAPYARD

S pectacular sight
C opper cars
R eally rusty
A pples ate
P layful place
Y ellow yachts
A wful Alsatian
R ich Rovers
D iced down.

Joshua Clarke (8)
St Chad's CE Primary School, Brighouse

THE RAT'S STORY

The sewer is my home,
The giant people moan,
They attack me, try to kill me,
With food try to tempt me.
They call men with strange liquid
That makes me go funny inside,
That is how my best mate died,
They really hate me.
They got a cat that almost ate me,
I hope we'll learn to get along,
By that time I'll be gone.
I am a small grey cloud,
Moving swiftly through the sky.

Luke Friis (10)
St Francis RC School, Bradford

HARRY HAMSTER HIRST

I listen very well to what people say,
I can go very fast,
I have a good home to live in,
My favourite food is lots of vegetables and greens,
My best time is when I run like a bullet
In a ball or a wheel,
I have small, white and ginger hair on my little body,
You might think I am defenceless,
But I have sharp teeth,
I live in a cage, alone,
When I'm in a new area
I take my time to get used to the atmosphere around me,
Then I sleep like a squirrel in hibernation.

James Hirst (10)
St Francis RC School, Bradford

THE FLUFFIEST RABBIT

Hello, my name is Fluffball
I am like a very big ball of fluff
I have very big teeth
I have a white coat with black spots
Please look after me, I'm all
Alone and foxes may come and get
Me and I haven't had a
Carrot in days, so please
Please look after me.

Olivia Leigh Cranmer (8)
St Francis RC School, Bradford

The Cat

I am cute and cuddly,
I get very muddy
And I always get fed.

Me and my family play together,
They give me a warm bed,
When it's morning I'm awake.

I was a small tiger,
Now I'm a big tiger who climbs curtains,
But I never scratch my family.

My favourite food is chicken,
People let me run around in their garden,
My colour is black and a bit of white.

I sleep in my basket next to the fire,
And make myself tired . . .

Night-night.

Emma Wilkinson (9)
St Francis RC School, Bradford

Poem About A Tortoise

I try my best, I do, I do,
But people just think I am as fast as I do,
I wish they'd listen; I'm as fast as a bee,
No, wait a minute, I'm no wee nor a bee.

When I waddle on the ground
All of a sudden I hear a loud sound,
I look up and all I see
Is just a very big door.

I tried to escape, I did, I did,
But all I could do was sob like a pig,
I wish I was bigger and a lot faster,
But all I can do is linger in laughter.

I live near a river, which is all so wet,
But sometimes I wish I was a warm house pet,
Sometimes I wish I could fly,
But I would not like to go too high!

Adam Butler-Fagbohun (10)
St Francis RC School, Bradford

THE FROG

I hop around like I don't know what,
From lily pad to lily pad, on a lovely day.

I'm as fast as a shooting star,
People say I'm a bouncy ball
And when I stretch my legs out far,
I'm very, very tall.

I'm small in size
And green in colour,
I eat flies for dinner,
Plants for supper
And blood for my lovely tea.

I swim around
In my little pond,
My big long tongue
It's very young,
I was only born last summer!

Christopher Doonan (10)
St Francis RC School, Bradford

CAT

I am a cat
all fluffy and fat.
I have a tail as pointed
as a nail.
I am black and white
so I can keep out of sight.
Watch out,
I might give you a fright!

Mice, mice, mice,
that sounds kind of nice.
I sip my milk out of a bowl
lined with silk.
I have a collar with a diamond stud on it
but I still like to play about in the mud.
Most of all I love my bed
where I can lay down my lazy head.
That's it for now,
miaow, miaow.

Megan Harper (9)
St Francis RC School, Bradford

THE TIGER

I'm swift crawling;
Forever stalking,
Precious as gold,
Never very cold.

I live in the jungle,
Love to mumble,
Like the grass,
Or apple crumble.

People hunt me because they are scared,
But some people like me because I'm rare,
I'm crafty, shifty, like a challenge,
When my prey comes I'll definitely manage.

I'm black, orange, white and grey;
In my home I'll relax and lay,
I like my food, every bit,
I like my colours to shine and be lit.

Michael Friis (8)
St Francis RC School, Bradford

THE CAT

I am a cat that is a fluff ball;
I am soft and gentle,
I am different colours like a rainbow.

I don't bite!
I move slow like a tortoise,
I live in trees and other places.

I miaow instead of woof;
I don't bite!
I like cat food and mice.

I am loveable;
Not sly and cunning,
Just the sort of way I like it.

I am reliable;
Never silly
And that's me!

Marco Rudak (9)
St Francis RC School, Bradford

DUDLEY THE DOG

My nickname is Chicken Guzz,
I've got a sister called Floss,
I eat Butcher's tripe mix,
People think I am cute,
People like to stroke me.

I always run when I hear the words,
Pussy cats, squirrels, walkies, pussy cat patrol,
People say I walk like Slinki from Toy Story,
When I am asleep I snore,
I stand on two legs and beg.

My footsteps are like a lion running,
I have to go now,
I'm going on a walk.

Laura Slack (10)
St Francis RC School, Bradford

THE DOG

I move very fast
With my white and black coat.
Yet you people think I am danger,
I suppose I was ready for a battle or at least a fight.
Terror is what I know best,
I chase cats but do not kill them
But I tell them, 'Stop teasing me
Or I will kill you.'
The good thing about people
Is they take care of me.

Thomas Heap (9)
St Francis RC School, Bradford

THE RABBIT

I hop around the garden all day
Then when I'm tired; I lie on hay.
My house is a hutch in your back garden,
When I'm hungry I eat lettuce and carrots.

I've long thick fur to keep me warm,
I sometimes live on a farm.
I've got long droopy ears and
When I'm hungry I'll nibble carrots
With my sharp teeth.

My fur is a silver grey colour,
With a white bushy tail,
I'll hop forward slowly to see
What you've got,
Then I'll stare straight at you
Waiting for more.

Alexandra Bolland (9)
St Francis RC School, Bradford

SUN

Why are you always hot in summer, sun?
Why do you make us dehydrate, sun?
Why do you stay in the Caribbean, sun?
Why don't you visit us in January, sun?
Why do you only come in summer, sun?
Why do you trail in front of spring, sun?
Why do you send a heatwave in summer, sun?

Because it's my job.

Lauren Robbins (10)
St Francis RC School, Bradford

THE LABRADOR DOG

I move like lightning
Cos I'm only a puppy
I can open a door to get in and out
I am never just lying about

When I want my food, I will jump like a baby elephant
When I get my food I sometimes eat like a pig
I can't possible taste the food
And my favourite is eating the kitchen.

I am supposed to be a man's best friend
But I can be your best friend
If you take care of me!

Nathalie Mannion (9)
St Francis RC School, Bradford

THE LIFE OF A FISH

Another day in the big bad world,
All day I'm on the move like a hiker, only in fear,
Just waiting to be caught.

I'm in constant danger of everyone all the time,
Yet I scavenge for any food left over.

Some food, no fish in sight this is my chance,
I've got it, but I'm racing,
I'm out of water, my life flashing before my eyes,
One last look at the world before it disappears
Forever.

Eddie Swales (11)
St Francis RC School, Bradford

MY CAT, DOMINO!

I walk around the kitchen
Looking for my food
When it's in my bowl
I woof it down in one
Then it's time for twelve hours nap
But I can never get comfy
Even though I'm funny.

When I wake up, I go out to play
I jump upon the gate
And play and play.

I want to come in with my muddy paws
With my fur like zebra skin
So I scratch down the door
But no one answers
So I run back over the garden
With my swinging belly and
With my muddy paws.

I finally get in with my muddy paws
And I lick my black and white fur
To get the mud off my muddy, muddy paws.

I'm vicious, warm and loving after a hard day's work
I want a human's hand to rub my chin
I look at them with my eagle eyes
Because the night's drawing in
I snuggle down in the big soft chair
And wait till morning comes.

Laura Frances Sheerin (11)
St Francis RC School, Bradford

POEM OF A MONKEY

I climb up trees,
when there's a cold little breeze,
but I'm so hairy that I don't freeze.

I eat fruit a lot of the time,
but the one thing I hate is a sour lime,
when I climb up trees I sometimes see slime.

I'm a bit like a human but a bit more scary,
I eat fleas
and I'm a bit more hairy.

I'm as flexible as a gymnast,
I jump tree to tree, so very fast
and for me there's no need for a weather forecast.

I can climb so very high,
but not quite as high as the birds can fly.

People think I'm very rough,
but really I'm as soft as fluff.

I make buddies with big gorillas,
now that's what I call big killers!

Myles Nesbitt (10)
St Francis RC School, Bradford

BRUNO

My name is Bruno,
I am a bull terrier-cross,
I don't know when whining,
Because I'm always shining.

Me, I can run very fast
And I'm a very gentle one.
I am as tough as a lion
And I'm as strong as a bull.

Sam Hannam (10)
St Francis RC School, Bradford

THE DOG

Sometimes I'm just a blur
Because I'm fast at running
Just like lightning
With a look that's frightening

I bark at bald men
Although I'm man's best friend
My fur is long and silky
Black and white's my colour

When you're kind to me I lick your face
When I'm hungry, feed me dog food or biscuits
Not too much because I will get tummy ache
In the night I stay awake

While in the day I slumber
In my dog basket I will sleep
Or on your settee will do
But don't let your dad find out
Or I will be put out

Please look after me
Because I do love you.

Gemma Fisher (10)
St Francis RC School, Bradford

THE LION

I am a fast orange monster,
Chasing after my prey
And when I catch my food
I tear it apart with my sharp claws,
Which swoop down at the speed of light,
To rip and eat my meal.

My bellowing roar is like a clap of thunder,
Hitting the ground on a dark night.
I am the king of the jungle,
Even though I do not mean harm,
But if you harm me I will attack.
My sharp teeth like razors will rip you apart
Until you are food for our pride.

It is my job to protect our pride,
My sleek look and my colour like an orange sunset
Must be protected for later generations,
And all my jungle is being destroyed
And soon I will have nowhere to live,
Then all my kind will have gone.

Matthew Smith (10)
St Francis RC School, Bradford

CAT

My name is Tigger
I have whiskers as long as giants' legs
I love milk and tasty meat
As I wander around
My tail and eyes look proud
I'm king of the house

My plan for a day is to eat and sleep
And wake up only for my food
I love a cuddle now and again
As long as you don't tease me.

Purr . . . purr . . . purr!

Fiona Nolan (11)
St Francis RC School, Bradford

FELIX

My name is Felix
I am soft and cuddly
My favourite sport is football
I run like David Beckham
Catch like a lion but
I'm still very friendly
I act like a tiger
My owners are nice
They cuddle and love me
Like a sort of teddy bear
I'm black and white
With a soft pink nose
I look like the cat off TV
He's called Felix too
Some people say
I pounce like a puppy dog
My favourite drink is milk
I've got a high tree to climb
I'm a cat but . . .
I still love my life.

Chantelle Craven (10)
St Francis RC School, Bradford

THE KITTEN

I'm playful when you get to know me
But I'm sleepy and weary at night
I wrap myself up in a blanket
You can turn off the night light
I'm tiny, sweet and loveable
I'm small and as furry as a ted
I am nervous and I am shy
But I'm still wild and frisky inside
You see that I like to eat
And my very favourite dish is meat
I clean myself neatly
I won't make a mess
My family are all bigger than me
They prowl around the jungle
But as for me
I don't, I just want to be your pet.

Bethany Atack (8)
St Francis RC School, Bradford

MY NAME IS DARCY

My name is Darcy
I like to eat
I like to get mucked-out every day
I am just white
I always get up early
I like to be clean
And to be washed and brushed
I like to be ridden all the time
But most of all I like to be loved.

Lorna Stokes
St Francis RC School, Bradford

THE CHEETAH

I'm a cheetah, cunning, fast and sly,
In the long, green grass I lie.
I'm found in zoos, safari parks,
Jungles and deserts.
I stalk,
When I catch my prey,
I slowly walk.
They can't see my camouflaged coat.
I catch my prey and bite their throat,
Then when they're dead, I eat them up.
They have a big gash and a deep, deep cut.
Antelopes, birds and rodents I eat,
I have a grin, it's my favourite treat.
I run around all day long
And when night comes,
I'm slowly gone.

Lindsay Parnham (11)
St Francis RC School, Bradford

KOALA

I live in forests and climb gum trees,
I'm a cuddly bear, I'm one of my own species,
I'm bigger than a female, medium in size,
I have a smooth nose and pearls for eyes.
I'll walk really slow,
I'll rub against your skin, I'll love you to bits,
Did I mention, I live in Australia?

So come visit me, you'll have a really good time,
But you better not make a gum out of me.

Luke Flacks (11)
St Francis RC School, Bradford

PANDA

I am a panda eating bamboo
My kids like it and I do too
We are some of the only ones left
What ones? A panda, yes, yes, yes.

I search the forests of China
For meat-free food
I find bamboo and eucalyptus
Mmm, it tastes good!

I am black and white, wow
Please don't shout, now
If I'm around, look!
My fur's as black as night
With patches of snow white

My kids play about, lots
Of fun and games
And rough and tumble
I say let them play

But we are becoming
Extinct, we are dying
Stop the forests being
Knocked down
Don't stop trying

Chinese forests are our home
Here, right here
Pandas now are really rare
I think the end is near

We run and climb for our lives
The kids can't play and dance
How come these humans
Never give us a second chance?

Daniel Murgatroyd (10)
St Francis RC School, Bradford

A GORILLA'S FEELINGS

I move like a human
A fierce man-like creature
But humans are my enemy
They hunted down my family
Wife, child, Dad and Mum
My only family are my adopted mum and dad.

I am a lonely creature
A beast to some of you
But if I bump into one more human
The first I kill is you!

I eat green leaves
And monkeys' fleas
The first I eat is
You!

Benjamin Houlbrook (11)
St Francis RC School, Bradford

ELEPHANT

I am an elephant, big and grey
hiding in the trees
in the wind my trunk will sway
in the soft and gentle breeze.

I am hiding from those humans
who want to kill me
but I'm going to put up a fight
to save my ivory.

Sometimes I wish I wasn't an elephant
oh so big, oh so grey
I wish I could change my life
in every single way.

Georgia Narey (11)
St Francis RC School, Bradford

CAT

I am a house animal
Although I do like the outdoors
Eats meat and I like a fire
Enjoy playing with a few toys
I enjoy plenty of love and attention
I also enjoy a stroke
I chase mice away
I love a drink of milk.

Rachael Bland (10)
St Francis RC School, Bradford

A Dog

I like to jump really tall
And dig with my paws,
My master is very nice to me,
He likes me, you see.

I like to live in a comfy place,
Something that's right for me,
I love to eat something that's good,
Something that's from the book.

I run very fast,
Then I go for a nap,
Then I smell food,
Then I stand up and go across the room.

Nicholas Doyle (10)
St Francis RC School, Bradford

Cat

I like to eat and sleep
I eat cat food and drink water
I am a ball of fluff
When I am lonely I go to sleep on the chair
People love to stroke me
When I go outside I go across the road
To see my friends.

Emma Dickenson (9)
St Francis RC School, Bradford

A SHEEP

I am a furry little creature,
Although I cannot swim,
I have a red cross on my wool
And the butcher calls me Tim.

I live on a farm
With all my other friends,
I love to eat grass,
Although things are tense.

I have a very high-pitched voice
And it goes like *baa baa!*
So now you've heard about me,
I'll have to say ta-ta.

James Lencki (11)
St Francis RC School, Bradford

MY DOG POEM

I jump around when someone passes,
I walk one leg at a time,
I wiggle my bum when I walk,
I bark when I want to go out
Or I want some food,
When I am hurt, I limp,
My type is a male boxer dog,
Sometimes I am good,
Sometimes I am bad.

Rory Doyle (9)
St Francis RC School, Bradford

The Elephant

Elephant hiding in the trees,
Animals fleeing everywhere,
Man with guns and scraggy hair,
The elephant is endangered.

'We'll chop off his tusks!'
They shout 'We'll be rich!'
They don't know what they're doing,
They only think of themselves.

'The feel of his skin, nice and rough,'
'The lovely feel of his lovely long tusks!'
'This is a big one!'
'It weighs 5 tonnes!'

'Here comes the herd!'
'Guns at the ready!'
'We've got quite a few'
'We're lucky we got any.'

Elephant looking from the trees,
Everything's gone quiet.
Man with guns and long, long hair,
Making a silent exit.

Blood on the ground,
The smell of gun powder,
A baby elephant stands on its own,
Most of the herd was taken.

Georgina Lennon (11)
St Francis RC School, Bradford

ABBY

Hi, my name's Abby
My coat is a golden colour
I run around all day long
It's as fun as fun can be
My owner is my best friend
I think I run even faster
Than a rocket going up to the sky
I'm intelligent and a perfect gentleman
But if I get bored . . .
I'll run around and start to claw the doors.

Alexandra Cansfield (10)
St Francis RC School, Bradford

SAM THE SNAKE

I am a snake, my name is Sam
I have teeth like a vampire
Rats, mice, hmmmm
I'm dry, not slimy and
I attack very, very quick and I'm scaly

Black and red, the pattern on my back
Rattle rattle goes my tail
Poisonous as a black widow
Cousins, turtle, tortoise and other snakes.

Nicky Hardaker (10)
St Francis RC School, Bradford

A Dog Called Lucky

I'm friendly and cuddly,
People love to play with me,
But when I'm bad
My owner smacks me.

I'm quiet all the time
And children think I'm fine,
I eat all the time
Even though I always whine.

I run around all day,
Because I love to play,
I jump like a kangaroo,
Even though I love you.

I'm very soft
And I sometimes have to sleep in the loft,
I'm very small
And good at climbing walls.

I eat all the food
And always like a treat,
But when I ask rudely, I get a big beat.

So now I'm home at last,
Nicely snuggled up in my bed,
I love to cuddle my big ted,
I'm now glad I'm warm in bed.

Rachel Noble (11)
St Francis RC School, Bradford

I'm Mitsy The Rabbit

I'm a rabbit who eats all day and night
Go out in the garden to play with my ball
My teeth are like razors
I will always be good
So I can get a carrot for a treat
My name is Mitsy
My coat is grey and white
I have a small mouth
Just like a pen lid
I run around all the time
My owner feeds me every day
And I need cuddling to keep me friendly.

Matthew Taylor (9)
St Francis RC School, Bradford

The Rat

You don't see many of us!
We normally hide in sewers!
I have a tail like a worm!
Which makes people scream and squirm!
You may think we're awful creatures!
When you get to know us and feed us now and again
You'll find we're very nice!
We hate cats!
We hate dogs!
We're rats!

Rachel Capuvanno (11)
St Francis RC School, Bradford

Sun

The sun is shining everywhere, are you there?
Yes I am.
Why do you shine so bright?
I am the sun, I'm supposed to shine so bright.
You are so shiny, why?
Because I'm supposed to shine.
Where are you?
I'm up here in the sky, why?
I just can't see you!
You can, I'm right in front of you.
Oh yeah, I can see you now.
What's your name?
I don't have one.
Why do you shine all over us?
So you have bright shining light.
Why can't you stay all day, day and night?
The moon my friend has to come out to get you to sleep.
I have to go now, it's my tea time.
Then go to bed.
OK see you tomorrow, by the way what's your name?
My name is Sarah.
OK, bye Sarah.
Bye sun.
See you tomorrow Sarah.
OK, bye.

Chloe Dores (9)
St Francis RC School, Bradford

Monkey

I may be soft and cuddly,
But I can be quite fierce,
I like to eat bananas,
Up high in the trees.
I can swing like an athlete,
Going for Olympic gold,
Sometimes I fall and hurt myself,
But I will soon recover
And be climbing in the trees again.
Before you know it,
I'm asleep.

Rebecca Brown (10)
St Francis RC School, Bradford

Rabbit

I am a little rabbit,
I am only lonely,
I only have one friend called Hare,
People often stare at me and Hare.

We do dares together and try to make new friends,
I only eat 1 carrot a day,
I am only 10cm wide and 16cm long,
I only want a home, that's all I ask for,
Please help!

Jessica Farrell (10)
St Francis RC School, Bradford

THE FRUIT BAT

I am the largest
Of my family,
I glide like an eagle,
But I am a bat.

So much fun,
When I fly through the sky,
I eat leaves and fruit,
But I also like flowers.

So if you see me,
Please put some out,
I am found in Africa
And also Australia.

Christopher Johnson (10)
St Francis RC School, Bradford

CAT

I am a cat, I'm called Heathcliff
and I am white and I've got black patches.
I have sharp claws, I live in a hut.
My hut has a fire in, I sit by it
and get nice and warm.

Sometimes when it's really cold,
I go inside and tickle my owner's feet.

Amelia Crossland (9)
St Francis RC School, Bradford

KENAN AND KEL

Kenan and Kel are so cool
even though Kel is a fool

Kenan is the leader of the gang
my favourite band is Wu-Tang Clan

I have a rat
my mum's friend is Pat

Kicking animals is cruel
even though I think it's cool

Manchester United rule
and my mum thinks I'm a jewel.

Jamie Douglas (11)
St Joseph's RC Primary School, Bradford

WINTER

W hen it's winter, my grandma comes to stay,
I n winter snow falls calmly for the day,
N o ice yet but I hope so, so that I can flow,
T rouble happens after all to all the children that fall,
E lves help Santa to fill his sleigh,
R udolf the red-nose reindeer helps Santa to deliver all the presents.

Nicole Holmes (8)
St Joseph's RC Primary School, Bradford

Sun And Plants

A sun has a glow, very hot,
Shiny and reddish,
It helps the plants grow in the pot,
When it's time to water the plant
Don't forget the sun did the lot.

When your plant is growing,
Help it by giving it lots of water
From the sky.

Always remember about the sun,
Because I said it's no one.

Emily Clark (9)
St Joseph's RC Primary School, Bradford

Billy The Clown

There once was a clown called Billy
He was very silly
He got a cat from his hat
How amazing was that?
He had little ants in his baggy pants
Billy danced and pranced
With a broom around the room
There once was a clown called Billy
He was very, very silly.

Ashleigh Brooksbank (10)
St Joseph's RC Primary School, Bradford

PIGS

I like pigs
they're really sweet
but others think
they're just to eat

Some are short
some are tall
like Gordy, Babe,
Piglet and all

Some are black
some are pink
some don't smell
but some sure stink

I like pigs
yes all kinds
like Gloucestershires, pot-bellies
and those with wacky minds

But the best pig
I like to boast
are the cute pot-belly
I like the most.

Daniella Baggio (11)
St Joseph's RC Primary School, Bradford

MY PUPPY

He is funny
Max, my puppy
He knows how I feel.

When I'm happy
He's so yappy,
Shrieks and squirms like a seal.

He knows when I'm mad
Because he looks very sad.

Max is so funny
Because he's my puppy.

Sarah O'Brien (10)
St Joseph's RC Primary School, Bradford

FAIRY TALES GOING WRONG

Once upon a time, in a forest far away,
Lived three little Goldilocks, who ate porridge every day.
As you can see, their names are all the same,
All because their mother couldn't be bothered with three names.
A bear came to visit from a village far away,
But the three little Goldilocks ate him anyway.
Then came their big brother, his name was Jack,
He liked to sleep in sleeping bags, toilets or a sack.
He owned a big blue beanstalk, that was shaped just like a fork,
It also grew so big, it led right into York.
Along came Cinderella, Cinderella was their mum,
She never cut her hair, so it grew right down to her bum.
Cinderella met a fella
And they were kissing in the cellar.
The name of this ugly man?
Well, his name was Peter Pan.
Then along came Wendy, Peter Pan's ex-wife,
She brought her three small children, an axe and a knife.
As she said to Peter, 'This is the end of your life,
Which one do you want? The axe or the large knife?'
But then the little children shouted, 'No Mummy, no.
We want to kill 'im, so just let go!'

Talitha M'Benga (10)
St Joseph's RC Primary School, Bradford

LIFE

Life started a long time ago
when people were born and they didn't even know.
Some people were big, some people were small.
Some people were medium or sometimes tall.
Some people have a good life, some people have a bad life,
as long as you go on thinking your life will change,
imagine your family being together again.
Imagine you're a pop star making lots of money,
there's always someone who has you in a hurry.
You see them on the telly, you think they're all that
but really they're just a cat trying to get out of the sack.
You see men and women arguing over something
but you don't know what it's about.
People get married, some get divorced,
some people live till they're 100 or 94.
Some people have kids that go to school, college even university.
Some kids have a good job that makes lots of money.
But that's life, it's worth more than money,
treasure it with your heart, don't give it to anybody!

Aimée Harrison (11)
St Joseph's RC Primary School, Bradford

SPRING

S   pring flowers bloom,
P   eople dance and sing,
R   ich golden sun shines in the sky,
I   n the night it's nice and warm,
N   ot everyone likes spring,
G   ot to have it, the way it comes.

Hayley Firth (9)
St Joseph's RC Primary School, Bradford

JOURNEY OF LIFE

J anuary was the month I was born,
O n the 27th of January, the year of 1991,
U nusually I had lots of hair,
R osy cheeks and a happy smile,
N ow I am nine, nearly ten,
E verything that has happened to me seems long ago,
Y oung and happy, looking forward now,

O ld I will be,
F or a happy life,

L ong and eventful,
I hope it will be,
F or me,
E lizabeth.

Elizabeth Peel (10)
St Joseph's RC Primary School, Brighouse

JOURNEYS

J esus will be with me wherever I may go,
O ver land and sea,
U p over mountains and down caves below,
R eminding me that he is there,
N ever going to be alone,
E ven if there's danger, he'll help me to get home,
Y our travels won't be lonely while he is there,
S o remember what I said and you'll be in his care.

Stephanie Lofthouse (10)
St Joseph's RC Primary School, Brighouse

GIANT

There was once a giant who was neither strong nor bold
By the looks of it he's very, very old
That very next day he was also told
You are really useless and just have to be sold

He's always watching telly
While eating cream and jelly
No wonder he's got a big belly
And that's not all, his feet are smelly

Poking at people's money
While eating bread and honey
Oh my gosh, he's really funny!
And now . . . look at his tummy

He's a bit of a joke
He's in for a soak
He's a silly bloke
When compared with other folk

An idiot he seems
But when it comes to jeans
He goes back to his teens
And eats lots of beans

His name is Bill
He's as big as a hill
His brother's called Phil
And he's always ill

Phil and Bill, the brothers
Don't think much of the others
But both do have mothers
And sleep under the covers.

I've learnt to rhyme
Just in time.

Adam James Foster (9)
St Joseph's RC Primary School, Brighouse

THE FOUR SEASONS!

Winter means snow,
Rain, sleet and hail,
Wind harshly blow,
Over hill and dale.

Spring means rain
And sun mixed together,
Water down drains,
Going down forever.

Summer means sun,
Holidays and camping,
Playing and fun,
All laughing and dancing.

Autumn means leaves,
Turn brown, yellow,
With a soft breeze,
Oh! How mellow.

Frances Tomlinson (10)
St Joseph's RC Primary School, Brighouse

THE WEIRD ZOO

I went to the weird zoo you see
It was so weird, I got in for free
But since the zoo was weird as you know,
There were cheetahs who were running slow.

Then I saw the monkeys
In the weird zoo as I've said,
In fact they were so weird
They were balancing on their head.

Then it was the lions,
Who didn't even roar,
Instead they started welcoming
Everyone they saw.

Then I saw the turtles
Who were extraordinary indeed,
Because it's rare that you see
Turtles with a cheetah's speed.

So I saw the hippos,
They were extra hyper,
In fact it was so strange
One was wearing a diaper.

Then I saw the emus,
Who I thought would be calm,
But I was shocked
When they started to read my palm.

Then I saw the giraffe,
Who had a long neck just the same,
But I was wrong about that,
When he said, 'Hi, Gareth's my name.'

Then it was the elephants,
Who were as dry as a bone,
But instead of eating peanuts

They choked on a stone.
So altogether there were . . .
Giraffes that were swinging in trees,
With necks that grew out of their knees,
There were elephants with humps
And camels with trunks
And a monkey that didn't have fleas.

Craig Lee (10)
St Joseph's RC Primary School, Brighouse

ANIMALS

I like animals, some are hairy,
Some are scary.
Bees surely aren't my favourite thing
Because they could sting.
Some are funny,
Like my bunny.
I like fish,
But not snakes that hiss.
I like pears,
So do bears.
I have meals,
So do seals.
It doesn't matter what they are, I still like all animals.

Gabrielle Greenwood (9)
St Joseph's RC Primary School, Brighouse

JOURNEYS

We take journeys every day,
As God guides us through life's way,
From young to old, small to big.

Journeys can be big or small,
As big as a holiday,
As small as up the hall.

Every small step is part of the journey of life,
It's all been a journey since you were a little tyke,
To know what we're all like.

Journeys can be easy or hard,
Big or small, short or tall,
Whichever one you choose to have,
Make your journey of life a safe one, not bad.

Sean McGeady (9)
St Joseph's RC Primary School, Brighouse

JOURNEYS

J ourney of life sometimes easy, sometimes hard
O ften funny, sometimes sad
U ps and downs with good and bad
R easons to be happy
N o time for regrets
E very day a new beginning
Y esterday has come and gone
S unrise begins a new day.

Luke Cowling (10)
St Joseph's RC Primary School, Brighouse

ANIMALS

Slugs and snails
Tigers and rats
Fish and whales
Birds and bats

Lizards and snakes
Insects that crawl
Lions and drakes
Hamsters in balls

Cats and dogs
Birds that fly
Bugs under logs
And owls that cry

Animals, animals
Everywhere
On the ground
And in the air.

Scott Morris (8)
St Joseph's RC Primary School, Brighouse

JOURNEY

J umping for joy, our holidays are here,
O ver the blue sparkling oceans we fly.
U p into the sky, to a country unknown,
R ays of sunshine glisten onto the water.
N eat little houses pink, blue and white,
E very night we hear the cricket's song.
Y ellow beams of sunshine in our room.

Emma Hempenstall (9)
St Joseph's RC Primary School, Brighouse

I Think About You

I think about you day and night,
When I'm with you it feels so right.
No one can see
How good it is to be me.

Jade Haley (8)
St Joseph's RC Primary School, Brighouse

Y4 Classroom

At school I shrank to 2cm tall
I was so, so terribly small.
The place was massive, gigantic, huge!
Just say it just like your shoes!

I know, I say it's so, so bright,
It can really brighten up the night.
I know it's hot,
But it's as hot as a pot!
Just say if you like this room,
Because it's nothing like a tomb.

Kate McBride (8)
St Joseph's RC Primary School, Brighouse

Wind

The grass is blowing
The doors of cars are banging
Branches are falling.

Kayleigh Harney (11)
St Joseph's RC J&I School, Castleford

In The Jungle

Lions, lions
They eat meat but
Tigers, tigers
Will catch you a treat!

Snakes, snakes
They eat anything, but
Sometimes wasps
Will give you a sting.

Monkeys, monkeys
Eat bananas and
Sometimes you get . . .
Bit by piranhas.

Lee Dawson (8)
St Joseph's RC J&I School, Castleford

The Ghost

He poked round the corner his head in his hands,
Patrolling up and down hissing demands.
The ghost stared around looking for help,
To make the new owner jump and yelp.

The ghost floated round him, his feet in the air,
He stared at him blankly - his squashed nose flared.
The owner looked at his watch for the time,
And said, 'My good fellow, it's nearly midnight.'

The owner closed his eyes and began to snore,
But the ghost gave up and walked through the door.

Afshan Naheed Lone (10)
St Joseph's RC J&I School, Castleford

SEVEN DAYS OF THE WEEK

At dawn on Monday
Frosty morning cold and dull
Children out with friends.

Cheerful Tuesday
Sparkling, shining morning
Makes me feel joyful.

Wet Wednesday morning
Children splashing in puddles
Soggy children play.

A stodgy Thursday
Seeing the sky going grey
That's today - Thursday.

A snowy Friday
Children building a snowman
Hailstone comes down.

Windy Saturday
Trees are whooshing in the sky
Children in their homes.

Scary day Sunday
Thunder and lightning scares me
People cuddle up.

Christina Sice (10)
St Joseph's RC J&I School, Castleford

COLONEL FAZACKERLY

He poked round the corner, his head in his hands
And stood upside down while shouting demands
Look, I'm a ghost, now why aren't you scared?
But Colonel Fazackerly just stopped and stared

The ghost floated round him, his feet in the air
He stared at him blankly, not fully aware
The colonel was bored now, gave a great yawn
He carried this on from dusk till dawn.

Daniel Smith (11)
St Joseph's RC J&I School, Castleford

THE PLANETS

Different planets near and far
Revolving round the sun!
Pluto, Neptune, Mars
Are you having fun?

On different planets there are different gods
Like Phoebe the great goddess
On different planets, different craters
All with different names.

Small planets, big planets, tiny planets
Uranus, Saturn, Venus too
The big black spot on Jupiter
A hurricane without a name!

Sarah Crossland (7)
St Joseph's RC J&I School, Castleford

JANUARY SEA

January sea
is as cold as Arctic snow
. . . frothing waves crashing.

William Delany (10)
St Joseph's RC J&I School, Castleford

THE OLD WOMAN CALLED DINA

There was an old woman called Dina
She came from a place called China
She had a big wagon
Was eaten by a dragon
That was the end of old Dina.

Lutangu Sando (10)
St Joseph's RC J&I School, Castleford

ALL ABOUT TEACHERS

Teachers, teachers, there are so many.
They teach English and maths.
I like English best of all because we read poems.
I like teachers very much,
They are so polite in class.

Francine Hey (8)
St Joseph's RC J&I School, Castleford

GOING ON HOLIDAY

Holidays are great!
You can't wait
We go on an aeroplane
We are going to Spain!
Spain is hot,
Oh no I've forgot . . .
What?

Paige Tomlinson (8)
St Joseph's RC J&I School, Castleford

THERE WAS AN OLD MAN FROM SCARBOROUGH

There was an old man from Scarborough
Who walked about on the harbour
But he fell in
And wrinkled his skin
That soggy old man from Scarborough.

Richard Dye (10)
St Joseph's RC J&I School, Castleford

THE ROCKET

The rocket is going
As if it was growing.
It's whizzing and twirling as if it was Merlin.
It's in the air, it's zooming through meteors,
As if it was a steam train.
The rocket is landing, the people are bouncing
And aliens are pouncing.

Adam Hetherington (10)
St Joseph's RC J&I School, Castleford

THE TRAIN JOURNEY

Here is a field full of fluffy white sheep
Stood by their owner little Bo Peep
Through the tunnel as she goes
Huffing and puffing away she blows
Down into the valley as she descends.

Dale Turner (10)
St Joseph's RC J&I School, Castleford

POINTLESS HAIKU

What am I doing?
I don't know what I'm saying
Really, what's the point?

Philip Leigh Newman (11)
St Joseph's RC J&I School, Castleford

THE GHOST OF THE OLD MAN

One winter night the old castle was sold,
To a man who was made completely of gold.
One night while waiting to go and eat,
He heard someone playing a ghostly beat.

He crept round the corner to see who was there,
To his amazement stood up his hair.
For what he saw was no less than a ghost,
'I'm here to haunt you and be your host!'

Stephanie Hetherington (11)
St Joseph's RC J&I School, Castleford

WINTER

Softly falling snow
Landing gently on the ground
Sound of crunching snow.

Kyle Boyle (10)
St Joseph's RC J&I School, Castleford

THE FLAMING ROCKET

The rocket flaming into space
And roaring and zooming, whooshing and rushing,
Blasting, whizzing and zooming,
A meteorite comes plunging along,
The rocket crashing and smashing into it,
The rocket banging and booming,
As if it was exploding.

Aaron Robinson (10)
St Joseph's RC J&I School, Castleford

AUTUMN

Autumn leaves falling . . .
softly descend to the ground
contrasting colours.

Louise Forster (10)
St Joseph's RC J&I School, Castleford

FROM A TRAIN CARRIAGE

Here is a pond full of white ducks,
Fast little child carrying some books.
The trees are blowing from side to side,
It's cold and blowy and windy outside.
Here are some houses that look like mixed pastels,
We are whizzing past old bent castles.
People are laughing loudly together,
Each a glimpse and gone forever.

Nicola Louise Newman (10)
St Joseph's RC J&I School, Castleford

THE STORMY OCEAN

The sea comes rolling in,
Smashing against the rocks,
Pushing itself, filling every gap,
Crashing into the docks,
Wrecking the boats,
Curling around,
Forcing them, whizzing them onto the ground,
The waves are clashing and lashing,
Destroying everything in their path,
Then the sea starts to calm,
It is dying to a soft gentle ripple,
Calming and softening,
Whispering its favourite song,
Hissing as it goes along.

Nicole Tracey (9)
St Joseph's RC J&I School, Castleford

A RAINY DAY

Stormy weather, stormy weather,
Rain dashing and splashing
And crashing to the ground.
Flooding and muddying the road.
Clashing on the pavement,
Jumping on umbrellas,
Wetting everyone's clothes.
Thundering and lightning,
Destroying plants that are
Struggling to grow.

Mariella Tempera (9)
St Joseph's RC J&I School, Castleford

BAD WEATHER

The rain is bouncing down,
Like a rocket setting off,
You can hear the wind blowing,
Hissing and howling.
You can hear the wind screeching,
Thundering and lightning.
You can even hear the devil,
Screaming with laughter
As the flowers are burning,
The fences are being wrecked,
A dog is barking,
The sunlight sky is sparkling.

Steven Adey (10)
St Joseph's RC J&I School, Castleford

DAYS

Snowy, Monday morn
Screaming through the wind, so cold
Freezing all the cars.

Bitter Tuesday noon
Frightening - the wind blows cold
Snowing faster now.

Wednesday's wind blows
On a very chill morning
On a winter's day.

Jordan Rice (10)
St Joseph's RC J&I School, Castleford

A Stormy Sea

The sea is plunging along,
Crashing and clashing, attacking the rocks,
Bashing and splashing against the boats,
As if dominating the whole world,
Whispering and hissing,
Knocking down all the sandcastles,
As the sea was slapping against the walls,
The waves were destroying everything possible.

Ian Campbell (10)
St Joseph's RC J&I School, Castleford

Sea Blizzard

The sea, strong then crashes along,
Shouting and calling as if a lion roaring.
Its animals and plants around
Clashing and crashing,
Dominating and attacking,
Knocking and shattering.

Adam Brown (10)
St Joseph's RC J&I School, Castleford

The Dancing Ghost

I was up on the table doing my tap,
When suddenly the ghost burst into a rap.
'Oh my dear friend that is not the right sound,
Come with me and I'll spin you around.'

The ghost and the colonel were dancing together,
'Come on' said the colonel, 'you look under the weather.'
He pulled him on the table and grabbed hold of his hand,
'Come on' said the colonel, 'this is my favourite band.'

Lauren Robinson (11)
St Joseph's RC J&I School, Castleford

A MOURNFUL DAY

The rain pouring and smothering rocks,
Crashing, clashing as if cymbals smashing,
The wind screaming and destroying,
Snowing and sleeting, splashing and flashing,
Darkening and thundering, sparkling and gleaming,
Banging and blowing, echoing and hailstoning,
Water scurrying down grates.

Abigail Skinner (10)
St Joseph's RC J&I School, Castleford

SAVING EARTH

The rocket is blasting and roaring to space
Whooshing, whizzing, racing and chasing
Trying to destroy the meteor, zapping and dodging
And dashing, clashing and bashing
Firing, shooting and crashing
And braking and shaking.

Carl Flanagan (10)
St Joseph's RC J&I School, Castleford

Marine Life

Graceful blue dolphin
swimming in crystal blue seas
chasing and playing

Gigantic blue whale
splashing in Arctic waters
diving and jumping.

Becky Thourgood (10)
St Joseph's RC J&I School, Castleford

Black Beauty, The World's Best Horse

Black Beauty, the world's best horse is racing.
She is in front of everyone and is very fast.
She is leaping and dreaming that she is going to win.
She is dashing and she is going to win the race.
She has won the race and everyone is coming around her.

Rebecca Sice (9)
St Joseph's RC J&I School, Castleford

The Rough Stormy Sea

The stormy sea goes crashing and splashing
The wind goes howling and growling
The sand goes whirling and twirling
I wish I was in bed, snoring and sleeping

People on the beach go paddling
And sailing one of the sailboats.

Siobhan Coyle (10)
St Joseph's RC J&I School, Castleford

THE GALE AT SEA

The strong sea then whizzing along
Like a thousand race cars plunging along,
Attacking cliffs like hundreds of rockets,
Like needles piercing through a boat
And leaping over and over, spinning like a bottle
And whistling and howling and firing and blasting,
Lashing the boats like thunder,
Whirling, twirling and jumping like dolphins
Crashing like whales,
Hunting like sharks
And the raging sea keeps going on.

Joseph Quinn (10)
St Joseph's RC J&I School, Castleford

THE WIND, THE SEA AND SKY

The wind whooshing and gushing,
Up rushes the storm, roaring through,
The gale whooshing on the pavements,
Wetting the street as the storm goes by,
Bad weather is approaching,
Rain, rain, whizzing through the
Dark, dark sky frightening, lightning,
Splashing, crashing, dashing, raining so fast,
Swirling and twirling as the
Whooshing night goes on.

Matthew Corcoran (10)
St Joseph's RC J&I School, Castleford

THE CRASHING OCEAN

The stormy sea mighty, then rages along,
Crashing and bashing as if glass smashing,
Its boats and ships destroyed,
Banging and clanging, dashing and clashing,
Shaking and roaring, shrieking and pouring,
Blazing and flickering, lightning flashing.

Threading and spreading, growing and flowing,
Bumping and jumping, thumping and hitting,
Pounding and bounding, splashing and thrashing.

Sharks and squids, whales and dolphins,
Waves go high, rocks go low,
Birds flapping, fish swimming,
The sea is rough and dangerous.

Matthew Williamson (10)
St Joseph's RC J&I School, Castleford

THE DEEP BLUE SEA

The deep blue sea chasing along when
the storm's pushing the sea around
and around and the deep blue sea
is splashing and crashing.

The sea is making loud noises
and huge waves, while everyone is
asleep and at midnight it quietens down.

Lauren Sims (10)
St Joseph's RC J&I School, Castleford

SPACE WARS

The space shuttle is on the take-off strip,
Tackling the runway quite easily,
Rapidly zooming through the sky,
Whooshing, flushing and rushing,
Breaking apart from the rocket like canisters
Revealing a laser gun,
Speeding, rushing, ripping and darting,
Dashing and streaking, blasting and tearing.

But then . . . disaster strikes,
Far across the galaxy an asteroid storm closes in,
Firing, shooting, blasting and launching,
Until all of the asteroids are destroyed.
Moving on, the space shuttle attacks the aliens' mother ship,
Bashing, booming, crashing and flashing fills the whole of space,
The Earth is now a safe place.

Joseph Brownridge (9)
St Joseph's RC J&I School, Castleford

SEASONS

Autumn leaves falling,
Lingering scent of moist leaves,
November morning.

A white frosty day,
Blizzards swirling fast and cold,
December evening.

Christopher Chilstone-Vause (11)
St Joseph's RC J&I School, Castleford

ALIEN CHASE

The rocket rapidly speeds along,
Blasting and roaring into space.
The rocket is zooming, speeding and booming,
On a great alien chase.
The alien's spaceship firing and shooting,
Destroying everything in sight,
Whizzing and dizzying around and around,
Crashing and dashing and banging and bashing
And then . . . silence.

Matthew Cogan (9)
St Joseph's RC J&I School, Castleford

THE SEA STORM

The sea is rough and tough,
It wishes and swishes around the shore,
The boats are rocking and swaying,
The sea is thundering and blundering
And whispering and hissing,
The sea is swaying and playing
And the wind is zooming and booming,
The sea is crashing and bashing,
Whilst a boat in the distance is sailing,

Joshua Marcus Gray (10)
St Joseph's RC J&I School, Castleford

ANIMALS

Some animals are cute
Some animals have fur like a cat or a dog
Some animals can be pets
Some animals live in the wild
Some animals have four legs
Some animals are big, some are small
Some animals have ears
Some animals are friendly
Some pets like being around people
We shouldn't be mean to animals
You can have your own pet but always take care of them
Animals count too.

Charlotte Slater (9)
Westville House Prep School

AGE OF EMPIRES

Age of Empires is really cool
Some explorers are fools
I like using cheats
I can do amazing feats
I can blow things up
Out of his hand would go the emperor's best drinking cup
Battles would rage
So we turn the page
To see what enemy there is next
I sometimes have to read the text
To make my plans go right
In case there is a fight.

William White (8)
Westville House Prep School

The Secret Murder!

There is a secret murderer
In a secret town
He murders people now and then
He stole King Charles' crown
He always gets away with it
He's always got a chance
He tries to set his brain on us
Well then . . . he's ready to dance

There is a secret murderer
In a secret town
Now he kills the whole wide world
I really hope he'll drown
His ears, his face
Well now that news will trace
And that's the secret murder
Good grace!

Kirsten van Terheyden (8)
Westville House Prep School

Ghosts

Ghosts are very scary I know
there're lots of places that are just 'no go'
they float around graveyards and haunt houses
they have white sheets, not shirts or trousers.

I went in a haunted house just the other day
it was dark, bleak and very grey
I was quite nervous but I kept aware
I heard groans and moans as I crept upstairs.

I began to feel quite scared
What am I doing? Does anyone care?
I think I'll creep back to my safe home
that will teach me never to roam.

Sam Ashton (8)
Westville House Prep School

RAPPING ANIMALS

I am a mouse
And I live in a house
I like to please
And I love my cheese.

I am a bug
And I live in a rug
I like my food
And I love to groove.

I am a bat
And I live in a flat
I feel so good
When I suck some blood.

I am a fox
And I live in a box
I jump the pen
And I kill a hen.

I am a mole
And I live in a hole
I scratch and squirm
Till I find a worm.

Harry Fisher (9)
Westville House Prep School

Who Does It?

Who does the mopping
After our weekly shopping?
Who goes loony
After we see Mr Mooney?

Who was born in May
Like Uncle Grey?
Who runs round our town
At dawn?

Who bounces our ball in our hall?
Who gets fed in bed?
Who tries to destroy our shed?

Who made bullies mean?
Who kicks me without being seen?
Who splats mud in my pud?
Who made cows moo?
To tell you the truth
I think it's you!

Ayman Khokar (8)
Westville House Prep School

My Mum Wants A New Car

It's done too many miles
The bumper's gone all rusty
We are all smiles
New car would be nice.

The tyres are all worn out
The paintwork's gone all dull
Yes, we silently shout
Even the ashtray's full.

The pockets are full of litter
Someone's drawn on the back seat
It wasn't any of us
A new car would be neat.

Trouble is, there'll be no sweets
No drinks, ice cream or toys
For at least six months
In Mum's car.

Rebecca Barnes (8)
Westville House Prep School

I Saw A Madman Fly In The Clouds

I saw a madman fly in the clouds
I saw a bird walk on the ground
I saw a worm dig down deep
I saw a mole whizz along the ground
I saw a car with an eye of fire
I saw a devil with a tail
I saw a cat with four legs
I saw a chair all out flat
I saw a rug with a handle
I saw a mug with long ears
I saw a hare with a quick fin
I saw a dolphin which was flat
I saw a ruler with a sharp point
I saw a pencil spin around
I saw a bowl all hot with flames
I saw a cooker round and happy
I saw a snowman made of willow
I saw a cricket bat pink and green.

David Helliwell (9)
Westville House Prep School

Golf

Golf is fun
With a putter putting this way
And a driver driving that way
Up a hill, down a hill onto the green

In a pit, out a pit
Getting out of its way
The ball flies high into the sky
When the travelling is done, a hole in one.

The players enjoy their game
Walking like Tiger Woods
But their play is not the same
What a shame.

George Hardy (8)
Westville House Prep School

The Beach

As I lay down on the golden sand,
The sun shining down on my face,
Waves lap up against the shore
And I think, what a wonderful place.

Seagulls fly high up above,
Fish swim in the deep blue sea,
As I glance across the crowded beach,
There's nowhere I would rather be.

As the sun goes down, the air goes cool,
I know I will soon have to leave
This heavenly place, which makes me smile,
Will soon disappear like the breeze.

Matthew Riddell (8)
Westville House Prep School

MY LITTLE CHICKEN

I have a little chicken,
His name is Pat.
He eats all the food in the house
And chases after the cat.

He runs after my little yellow ball,
To find him I never have to call.
He likes to play with balls of wool,
But I wouldn't like to see him chased by a bull.

My little chicken is such a laugh,
But his jokes are really daft.
He mostly does as he is told,
Save to say when he has a cold.

Charlotte James (8)
Westville House Prep School

FOOD

Eggs taste better when they don't have legs
Jam is better when it's not on ham
What's inside apples leaves me baffled
You have to eat curry in a hurry
Don't eat beef with a leaf
Delicious steak makes the world shake
I think mustard is better than custard
Bread tastes better when its yeast is dead
Fish makes a nice dish
All green olives are quite solid
Prawn is better than a thorn
A juicy pear is better than hair.

Joseph Holloway (9)
Westville House Prep School

Johnny No One

His name is Johnny No One
He's all of 10 years old
He goes to school in Ikley
Now his story will unfold.

He's not in fact a boy child
He comes from outer space
And why he's here on Earth
Is to be part of the human race.

He comes from a planet called Stupond
That is far, far, far away
But now he is on Earth
It's where he wants to stay.

Alexander Raczkowski (9)
Westville House Prep School

I Saw A Clock Branching Out

I saw a clock branching out
I saw a rosebush scream and shout
I saw a madman fly up high
I saw a lark break and crash
I saw a wave bark at a cat
I saw a dog flowing swiftly
I saw a river trample on the turf
I saw an elephant write a word
I saw a pen lick its lips
I saw a baby laden with fruit
I saw a tree with wide-open eyes
I saw a horse playing with a ball
I saw the boy who witnessed these things.

Orlando St Clair-Charles (9)
Westville House Prep School

I Saw A ...

I saw a clock branching out
I saw a rosebush scream and shout
I saw a madman blowing bubbles
I saw a fish who had lots of luck
I saw a man read a book
I saw a pheasant who crushed a house
I saw a mouse squash a louse
I saw a girl shiver from toe to head
I saw a cat who lay by a tree
I saw a frog lying by a gravestone
I saw a mummy milking a dog
I saw a cow climb a tree
I saw a monkey wearing glasses
I saw a teacher used for signal flashes
I saw a torch that made this sight clear.

Kimberley Howard (9)
Westville House Prep School

I Saw A Madman Wrestle With A Gorilla

I saw a madman wrestle with a gorilla
I saw a cat play a violin
I saw a fiddler play the piano
I saw a granny kick a knight
I saw a horse ride a man
I saw a man jump on a hippo
I saw a lion eat a pizza
I saw a lady drive a racing car
I saw a professional break his leg
I saw an old man who saw this wondrous sight.

Jessica Jarrold (10)
Westville House Prep School

I Saw A Shark Scared Of An Ant

I saw a clock branching out
I saw a rosebush scream and shout
I saw a madman wrestling a fish
I saw a shark scared of an ant
I saw a grown man fight a lion
I saw a hyena on a boat
I saw a sailor floating in space
I saw an astronaut swing from tree to tree
I saw a gorilla mending shoes
I saw a shoemaker using bones
I saw a zoo using my loo
I saw the man who saw it too.
How about you?

Sam Macro (9)
Westville House Prep School

I Saw A Clock

I saw a clock branching out.
I saw a rosebush scream and shout
I saw a madman fly to Mars
I saw a space shuttle go to a burger bar
I saw a boy walk up a wall
I saw a spider ten feet tall
I saw a tree being picked up by a caterpillar
I saw a leaf taller than a miller
I saw a giraffe make a speech
I saw a politician destroy a whole beach
I saw a tornado fly a plane
I saw a pilot die and die again.

James Roulston (9)
Westville House Prep School

I Saw A Madman Fall Off A Cliff

I saw a madman fall off a cliff
I saw a rock squiggle and squirm
I saw a worm swim underwater
I saw a fish kill a squirrel
I saw a hunter make such a meal
I saw a chef crawl all around
I saw a rat play the piano
I saw a pianist fly in the air
I saw an eagle burn right to ashes
I saw a house break his glasses
I saw a blind man run 100 metres
I saw an athlete weigh 200 tons
I saw the thing that saw this sight.

Jonathan Baxandall (9)
Westville House Prep School

I Saw A Pig's World Turning

I saw a pig's world turning
I saw a boy in a pen
I saw a madman kick a van
I saw a monster roll down a hill
I saw a cow in a yellow mill
I saw a knight roll about
I saw a ball with a shield
I saw a child in the field
I saw a cat scream and shout.

Joseph Pointon (10)
Westville House Prep School

I Saw A Chicken With Long, Fleshy Legs

I saw a chicken with long, fleshy legs
I saw a madman lay brown eggs
I saw a tulip which tasted quite sour
I saw a lemon which looked like a flower
I saw a man without a tyre
I saw a car who was a liar
I saw the sun being called Sire
I saw a king like a ball of fire
I saw a man about to be sold
I saw a necklace who was very, very bold
I saw a frog that was neatly sewed
I saw a jumper that looked like a toad.

Calum Metcalfe (10)
Westville House Prep School

I Saw A Clock Branching Out

I saw a clock branching out
I saw a rosebush scream and shout
I saw a madman eating insects
I saw a frog swallow a goat
I saw a python chopping up wood
I saw a man squishing all the trees
I saw a boulder flying up high
I saw a rocket turn to a man
I saw an ape open and close
I saw a blind 30 metres deep
I saw a swimming pool eating a fish
I saw a man swallow a shark.

Clem McDowell (9)
Westville House Prep School

I Saw A Clock Branching Out

I saw a clock branching out
I saw a rosebush scream and shout
I saw a madman 100 feet tall
I saw a tower croaking loudly
I saw a frog pop with a bang
I saw a balloon as tall as a house
I saw a tree squirt out ink
I saw a pen shine out brightly
I saw a star watching TV
I saw a child flying up high
I saw a bird painted white
I saw a vase crawl along the ground
I saw an ant eating a sheep.

Richard Mason (9)
Westville House Prep School

I Saw A Madman Full Of Water

I saw a madman full of water
I saw a swimming pool burst into rain
I saw a cloud set on fire
I saw a bonfire ice over
I saw a pond made of brick
I saw a house fall over
I saw a glass slowly dying
I saw a rabbit milking a cow
I saw a farmer leaping a waterfall
I saw a salmon with a shiny dagger.

Harry Kirwan (9)
Westville House Prep School

I Saw A Pillow Eat A Hippo

I saw a pillow eat a hippo
I saw a man being milked
I saw a cow with lots of petals
I saw a flower go on a dog
I saw a rug six feet deep
I saw a flea sixty miles long
I saw a bath go up a chimney
I saw a fire drop down rain
I saw a storm coloured bright yellow
I saw a coat on a brass holder
I saw a candle eat a wire
I saw a puppy click a button
I saw a control full of peanut butter
I saw a jar made of bricks
I saw a house with a big screen
I saw a TV full of feathers.

Polly Goodall (9)
Westville House Prep School